SONNY DAYS

*The dark side journey of an undercover narc into
the light of community policing*

WILLIAM B. McCLARAN

WITH

FRANK O SMITH

Killarney Press
Portland, Maine
2014

Library of Congress Cataloging-in-Publication Data
McClaran, William B.
Sonny Days / William B. McClaran

ISBN: 1496020502
ISBN-13: 9781496020505
Library of Congress Control Number: 2014903686
CreateSpace Independent Publishing Platform, North Charleston, SC

MANUFACTURED IN THE UNITED STATES OF AMERICA

First edition

Spring 2014

DEDICATION

This book is dedicated to my daughters,
Pat and Lynn, and my son, Will.
Without their love, support, and encouragement,
this story would never have been told.

SONNY DAYS

PROLOGUE

The Dark Side

He pulled the gun and laid it on the low table between us. The clamorous sounds of downtown Detroit suddenly grew muted, amplifying the stillness that filled the room.

This fucking doesn't look good.

My eyes never wavered from his gaze, yet I knew the gun was a snub-nosed Colt .38. Not big, but very lethal, especially at close range. There was maybe eight feet between us. The odds of him missing me were damn near zero.

I mustered every ounce of my street persona as William "Sonny" Sonetti, the alter ego I inhabited as a federal undercover agent with the Bureau of Narcotics. I permitted no fear or surprise to register. I let a small sneer of disdain tug at the corners of my mouth, nodding ever so slightly as we stared at one another.

"That make you feel better, does it?"

He continued to eye me, forearms resting on his knees, his long slender fingers dangling loosely as he sat on the couch in his second-floor walk-up. He straightened but did not lean back into the cushions. The gun remained within easy reach. I had been in Detroit only a few weeks, but I knew he was a major player among heroin dealers. He wasn't physically big, but he was menacing enough—even before he pulled the gun.

"You say you know Philly," he said, appraising me coolly.

We sat opposite one another, the table and the gun between us. I didn't respond.

"Well, I know Philly," he said, a small smile lighting his dark face. "Let's you and me talk Philly."

I pursed my lips, giving nothing away.

Know Philly? Oh yeah. I knew Philly. I'd worked the streets of Philadelphia for a year and a half before being transferred to Detroit. The bureau didn't like to keep an undercover agent too long in any one locale. It wasn't conducive to his health. But in the eighteen months I was there, I came to know the seamier, darker side of South Philly: the rank, sour-smelling bars and juke joints where connections are made; the shadowy heroin "shooting galleries" where hardened junkies struggle to find a vein to tap. I knew the shabby, filthy streets where drug dealers take your money and disappear, then several minutes later send their five-year-old daughters back up the sidewalk with their little purses swinging, smiling as they come up to where you're sitting in your car, saying, "Hi, Sonny. My daddy told me to give this to you."

Oh yeah, I *definitely* knew Philly. In ways most people couldn't begin to imagine.

CHAPTER ONE

Stretching to Make the Cut

There was nothing in my childhood to indicate any interest in becoming a federal undercover narcotics agent. Nothing even to foretell a career in law enforcement. But looking back from the vantage point of now being out of active law enforcement and teaching criminal justice at the college level, I can see the fairly full arc of my life and can appreciate numerous small, seminal moments and experiences as a child and a young person that subtly bent my path in that direction.

I might have been a typical new recruit when I first started as a police officer, but I developed a reputation over time for going about things in my own way. I was viewed by some as radical, though I always strongly believed that my ideas and practices were rooted in common sense. As I advanced in my career, my approach didn't always endear me to local politicians and state authorities. I didn't much care. My actions were always grounded in a core set of personal values that determined how I did my job. They are now at the foundation of what I try to instill in my students, all so eager to serve, but few with real appreciation for the career or how it will dramatically affect their lives.

Being a cop changes you—all jobs do. The challenge in being a cop is to ensure that you do well in your career while also doing social good. Even when you walk on the dark side. The challenge is never to lose your way.

I was four when my father was called up from the naval reserves to active duty at the start of World War II. We were living in Grand Rapids, Michigan, at the time. Grand Rapids sits astride the Grand River about twenty-five miles east of Lake Michigan. It was known as the "furniture city" for the number of prominent furniture-manufacturing companies headquartered there. The Grand River Valley was first settled by missionaries and fur traders in the early nineteenth century and began to prosper soon after it was incorporated in 1850. Furniture making was long a part of its heritage.

My father was born in Indiana, raised in Ohio, and came to Grand Rapids to write for the *Herald*, the city's morning paper. He had volunteered for the navy back in 1917 and had served as a quartermaster on submarine chasers in the Gulf of Mexico, the Caribbean, and the Mediterranean during the First World War. After the war, he attended Ohio State University and received a bachelor's degree. He then joined the navy reserve and was commissioned as an officer. He was called up to active duty in 1940 to captain three different ships, the last the USS *Wiseman*, a destroyer escort, in both theaters during the war.

We lived in a two-story colonial on Benjamin Street north of downtown not far from the river. The house was big enough that "Bama," my grandmother, my mother's mother, gave up her apartment to come live with us when my father shipped out. She and my older sister, Joan, and I each had our own bedroom upstairs.

Though we had a car, it mostly sat in the garage, as gas rationing for the war effort was tight. Like everyone else, we didn't go out at all at night. After sundown, the city was in total blackout. No streetlamps were lit. We even had to keep our windows covered to prevent any wayward enemy planes that might penetrate the heartland from being inadvertently tipped off to the existence of life below, triggering a bombardment. When I grew a little older, I joined my mother, grandmother, and sister in their nightly Monopoly games that we played on a card table set up in the living room.

My mother was very warm and loving. She was also outgoing and had a lot of friends. On occasion, she would go out to the officers' club during the day to visit with other officers' wives, many her age and in the same circumstance with young children at home. Though there was much uncertainty to the times, the women supported one another while their husbands were overseas.

I have only the vaguest memories of my father before he returned from the war in 1946. The first thing he did was move us from Benjamin Street to Bostwick Lake, some twenty miles east, out in the country. Our house at Bostwick Lake was far less grand than our house in town. It was a simple, single-story structure that sat on a rise above the lake, amid other simple homes overlooking the water. I went to a one-room, one-teacher school for a year, mostly with farm kids from the area. The school had a wood stove for heat in the winter, an outhouse, and no running water. A black-and-white school photo I have shows a stern, stoic-faced woman who was our teacher standing with twenty-three kids assembled in four rows, the younger ones seated on low planks in front, the older kids standing on wooden risers in the back. The younger girls are all in gingham dresses, the older girls in skirts and blouses. The boys are dressed in ill-fitting pants—either too baggy or too short, with one boy in denim overalls. I'm standing in the middle of the third row up with a whistle on a lanyard around my neck, the "badge" of distinction that marked me as the school safety captain.

Bostwick Lake was good sized and a popular destination for people from the area and from as far away as Grand Rapids. There was a beach down at the far end, with a bathhouse and a popular hamburger stand. In the summer my sister worked there, and I was hired to do beach patrol. Lots of people came daily to go swimming. It cost a dime to swim, and my job was to patrol the beach to ensure that everybody paid. I, in turn, was paid the princely sum of twelve cents an hour.

In the winter, Bostwick Lake, iced-over and snow-covered, felt very isolated. The roads were plowed infrequently, but my father drove every day into town to work at the paper. Even during the summer it was fairly isolating, at least for my family. We never went anywhere; we never took a family vacation. I have no knowledge of what my father was like before the war, but after he came home he was very quiet, largely withdrawn into his own world of simple routines. Every evening after dinner he went out on the small porch that overlooked the lake to listen to the radio. Though my mother and I were very close, I can't remember ever having a substantive conversation with my father. I never came to truly know him.

I went to high school in nearby Rockford, where I played football. I was good at it, playing both offensive and defensive guard. Football was the only subject of interest that I shared with my father. He came to the games to watch me play, and later we would talk about how the game went and how I'd performed.

My dream was to play football for the Michigan State University Spartans. Though forever a long shot, it was the only vision I had for the future. I was elected at the end of my junior year to be co-captain of the Rockford Rams during my senior season. My imagination was lit with dreams of a great season to come.

One night that winter, during an intense cold spell, I was awakened by my mother's screams. My sister Joan and I ran to my parent's bedroom. My mother was sobbing over my father's body. He was dead, taken by a heart attack while sleeping. I distinctly remember the chill of the room, the sight of the two of them, my mother's grief so greatly animated, the utter stillness of my father lying on the bed in stark contrast. It's a memory vivid to me to this day.

Though it was still dark, dawn wasn't long off. My mother had me call the state police, who said they'd send out a unit. There were no house numbers at Bostwick Lake, so she told me to take the flashlight and go out and wait to flag it down. I remember standing out in the road as the night sky slowly grayed, shivering violently from the cold and the shock of my father's death. I was sixteen. He was only fifty-three. My father was buried with full military honors. After the service, one of his colleagues came over and told me solemnly "you're the man of the house now."

After my father died, we moved to Rockford. My grandmother came to stay with us. In moving my mother found a letter he'd written not long before he died. In it, he asked the navy to recall him to service for the Korean War. Though my mother knew that the Second World War had changed him, the letter was a complete surprise. It made her realize how deeply the war had affected him, so much so that rather than desiring to stay home with his family, he wanted to leave us and return to command a ship.

I managed to make the all-conference team my senior year, despite injuring my knee midway through the season. Getting injured sidelined my dream of ever playing for Michigan State. That spring my grandmother died. After I graduated, my mother rented a house in Grand Rapids, and she and my sister and I moved back to the city.

The next fall I started at Grand Rapids Junior College, mostly to play football. Though I was barely five foot ten, the coach assigned me to play fullback. I again injured my knee in the second game, ending for good my career in football. It changed the whole trajectory of my life. Things went downhill from there. I felt utterly lost during the fall of my second year. I skipped classes and stopped doing homework. Not surprisingly, my grades plummeted. That spring I flunked out. I was clueless about what I wanted to do. I felt a total failure. Though my mother was always supportive, I really had no one to talk to, no one to mentor me, no one to help me assess my options and select the best way forward.

I'd earlier joined the naval reserve the year after my father died. In April 1955, after flunking out of college, I signed up for two years of active duty.

No matter how many stories you hear, you can never be prepared for boot camp. Drill instructors take great joy in making the life of new recruits as miserable as humanly possible. I did basic training at the Great Lakes Naval Training Center in Illinois. It was my introduction to subjugation and brutality in the ranks, of men of greater authority lording their power over those with less.

There was a black recruit in our group who was targeted for special abuse from the first moment the drill instructors set eyes on him. This recruit was so intensely and unmercifully verbally assaulted in the first few days that he soon dropped out.

A few weeks later I happened to be walking down a hallway in the headquarters building when I passed an open door just as a drill instructor slapped a recruit across the face. When the recruit filed a complaint, I was surprised to find that he listed me as a witness.

The drill instructor wasted no time in confronting me. Cornering me alone, he threatened me. He told me if I knew what was good for me, I wouldn't testify in favor of the other recruit when the complaint came up for review.

"You'll never make it through boot camp. I'll see that you never pass inspection again," the instructor snarled. "I will *always* find something, the slightest smudge of dirt on your whites. You'll fail basic and won't be able to stay in the navy unless you go through basic all over again."

As it was, I regularly phoned home to talk to my mother. During the next call, I told her what happened. Ever sagacious, she told me not to worry. She said she would send me money to buy a second set of whites. I was only to wear them for inspections. I bought the second set and kept them carefully stowed in my locker. I did, in fact, manage to successfully complete the two-month basic training, and I began active duty.

I was assigned that first summer as a guard at the Great Lakes Naval Training Center. In the fall I was sent to Long Beach, California, to serve on the USS *Buckley*, a destroyer. Life was fairly monotonous, spent mostly out at sea practice firing the ship's guns. One day an executive officer asked a crowd of us if anyone knew how to type. "I can," I quickly volunteered. Without further questioning, I was reassigned to the ship's office, where I began to hunt and peck my way through the daily reports I was assigned to put out.

Eventually the ship got orders to go to sea for extended training. I didn't have much time left in my enlistment, so I was transferred to the USS *Frank E. Evans*, another destroyer. Soon after, the *Evans* got orders for Australia, and I was transferred again. This time I was assigned to shore patrol, where I was teamed with a marine MP to patrol parts of Los Angeles frequented by members of the military.

I got out of the navy in April 1957 and returned to live with my mother and sister in Grand Rapids. I was as clueless about what to do as I had been when I flunked out of college. I started studying the want ads. Two ads caught my eye. One was for a job working in one of the local manufacturing plants. And the other was for new recruits for the Grand Rapids Police Department. I applied for both without any preference for which job I preferred. The first one to offer me a job would get me.

I took the civil service exam for the police department and was surprised to get the highest score among the twenty candidates who took the test. I was pretty excited. But when I went for my physical, I was told that I didn't qualify. I was a quarter inch shy of the five-foot-ten-inch minimum height requirement. Department policy, however, permitted a second physical exam.

Though disappointed, I was far from deterred. If anybody ever told me I couldn't do something, it made me only more determined to prove the contrary. I enlisted my sister to help. We fashioned a weight out of a thermos filled with nails, which I strapped to my ankles while I hung from an overhead pipe in the basement. I went to the local Y, where a guy there told me that he'd be happy to help, suggesting he could hit me on the head with a wooden club to raise a bump that would give me the quarter inch I needed. I considered it, but decided that would be my last resort. I went to a chiropractor; he told me that when I went back for another physical, I should be sure to get measured first thing in the morning, and to have somebody drive me there so that I could lie down in the backseat to minimize any spine compression from sitting upright.

The day of my second physical, I had my mom drive me to the police station while I stretched out in the back. I went in and was measured. I topped out at five foot ten exactly.

I'll never know what my life might have been like if I'd first heard from the manufacturer where I had also applied for a job. And so began what would become my long career in law enforcement.

CHAPTER TWO

Ol' School Initiation

Grand Rapids was the second largest city in Michigan and had a large police force of some four hundred officers. As a new recruit, I went to the city's police academy for twelve weeks of training before I was assigned to a partner and permitted to go on patrol. At the time, I had no appreciation for how unique Grand Rapids was in requiring recruits to be put through extended training before letting them out on the streets.

I was eager to be a good cop. I had noble ideas about serving the public. I attentively took notes in classes, mostly instructed by senior officers lecturing on areas of specialty, and also by outside professionals who came in to speak on other topics, including law, the court system, and citizen rights. We were put through physical fitness training where I excelled, and training for how to handle volatile situations, such as dangerous encounters that involved a weapon. My training provided a good foundation at the start of my career in law enforcement; it was something I would value highly throughout my career.

After I graduated from the academy, I was put in a patrol car with a more seasoned officer on the night shift. I rode shotgun; he drove. It wasn't long into my first shift when we received a call from the dispatcher to respond to a complaint of a prowler in a neighborhood not too far away. We cruised past the address, and then we went around the corner to patrol the alley behind the house. Our headlights caught a black man standing in the alley with a piece of wood in his hand. My partner stopped abruptly and jumped out, commanding the man to put down the club.

"I'm the guy who called you."

"I don't care who you are. Put the fucking club down!" My partner stood with his nightstick drawn.

"But I called you," the man stammered.

"I said, put the weapon down. Or *you're* going down!"

I was taken aback. It seemed so unnecessary to respond as he had, even offensive to speak to the man as he did. The guy tried to explain.

"I won't tell you again. Put the fucking weapon *down!*" My partner had no interest in hearing another word until the man did as commanded. The black man was obviously upset, but eventually he did as he was told.

The resident told us he'd heard a noise outside and had called the police, then had come out, found a piece of wood, and began to inspect the area around his house. He'd just come out in the alley when we pulled up. The officer curtly directed him to go back inside. We made a cursory search and found nothing. We got back in the car and went back out on patrol. My partner said nothing by way of explaining why he had behaved as he had.

Later, we were cruising one of the city's main boulevards, one with a wide, grassy, center divider. My partner was driving far faster than prudent for no obvious reason. All of a sudden he lost control of the car, went up over the curb, and careened over the grass into the oncoming lane. Apparently the jolt of hitting the curb caused the windshield wipers to snap on. As we sat facing the wrong way in the far lane, he tried to shut them off, but couldn't. He got out, opened the hood, and ripped out the wiring for the wipers.

He got back in grumbling about defective parts. He was clearly distressed at losing control of the car. He put the car in reverse and did a half turn. Before putting it in first to start down the street properly, he glanced at me quickly. "If anybody asks—you saw how we got forced off the road. Right?"

Meekly, I nodded.

Late in the shift we got a call to respond to a murder. There were already several other officers on the scene when we rolled in. A black woman had been raped and murdered in her apartment. While we waited for the coroner to appear, the group of officers stood around the body of what had been a beautiful young woman who now was dead on the floor, her body almost completely naked. Various officers made comments about how "good" she looked, how sexy she was, sharing their fantasies for what they would have liked to have done with her.

Since my discharge from the navy and return to Grand Rapids, I had been staying at my mother's. She was already up fixing breakfast and had a cup of coffee waiting for me when I returned home from my shift.

"How'd it go?" she asked.

I was exhausted—physically and emotionally. "You wouldn't believe what happened," I said despairingly. "You just wouldn't believe it."

"Why? What happened?" she said alarmed, hearing the distress in my voice.

I shook my head. "It was *awful*." I sat down at the kitchen table and took a sip of coffee. She stood waiting. I shook my head in dismay. "I don't think I can do this. I don't think I'm cut out to be a cop. I need to quit and find another job."

My mother insisted I tell her what happened. She listened patiently while she prepared and set a plate of food in front of me.

She'd always been a good listener, supportive, and even a confidante at times during my younger years. She poured herself a cup of coffee and sat down to join me. When I finished telling her about the events of the evening, we sat in silence for a long moment.

"I wouldn't make any hasty decisions based on one night on the job," she finally offered. "I think you should sleep on it. You'll probably see things in a different light when you're rested."

Not surprisingly, she was right. When my shift rolled around late that evening, I put on my uniform and headed back downtown to report for duty.

It was an adjustment to work as a cop—bigger than I had anticipated. I had always seen doing police work as a public service. But there was a culture that I could not have imagined—nor could anyone else who didn't live it. It deeply colors how officers go about their jobs. Jobs that are—even to this day in this country—pretty thankless. Though most people whom police encounter on the job are good, decent people, officers witness the worst, the vilest of human nature as a matter of course. The only people who really understand what an individual officer goes through are other officers. It is a tight-knit group in an extremely high-stress job. To help deal with the stress, the work has its own dark humor—humor that when viewed from the outside can seem "sick." The humor, however, is really a coping mechanism. You belt up, put on the badge, and go out and do what has to be done. A lot of what you encounter isn't pretty. And as a consequence, officers build a psychic shield around themselves in an attempt to protect against letting the job get to them. But it does. It can't be helped. It's almost impossible not to take the job home with you, often with adverse consequences that get played out in rancorous family and interpersonal interactions—and worse.

On Mondays when we'd go in to start our shifts, the common joke was to ask how many prisoners were on "turban row." Turban row was where prisoners who'd been clubbed during the weekend were segregated and housed to recuperate. With their heads swathed in bandages, the several cells we used for those prisoners did in fact look like turban row.

Dark humor was but one distinctive aspect of the job. So, too, was intimidation.

After I had been on the job for a few months, I became cognizant of where the interrogation rooms used by the detectives were located. Each small room had two chairs. I happened to notice that in one room, the wall behind where the suspect sat was scuffed with numerous indentations. One day I asked another officer what had caused the marks on the wall. He explained that if an officer desperately wanted to get a confession, there was one detective you could call on to get the job done. He was a big, ugly guy—very intimidating. When he asked questions, he'd always have the suspect sit with his chair against the wall. If the detective didn't like the answer he got, he'd crack the wall next to the suspect's head with his blackjack. He was extremely effective at getting the answers—and the confessions—that he wanted.

Over the last century and longer, there has grown up a pervasive national subculture around this sort of thing. So much so that some of the slang that arose spontaneously many years ago has now become a part of mainstream culture. In New York City, for example, there was at one time a detective inspector by the name of Byrnes. He was always called in to handle the toughest cases, for he was widely known for being able to get confessions. When he interrogated a suspect, if he didn't get the answers he wanted, he'd beat them and lock them in a sweatbox, a small, airless, windowless room. Suspects with the misfortune of being interrogated by Detective Byrnes were referred to having undergone the "third degree"—a pun on the detective's name. The term is commonly known today—but with little or no understanding or appreciation of its origins.

One time my partner and I were bringing in a suspect who sat in the backseat in handcuffs. I was driving. When the suspect leaned forward to ask a question, my partner swung his nightstick and cracked the guy on the head, breaking open his scalp, sending the man wailing against the backseat, writhing in pain. With his face covered in blood, the suspect finally managed to ask why my partner had hit him. "Just shut up and stay back where you're supposed to," the officer said. "And don't ask any more questions."

There was another tactic that was applied by some officers in similar situations. It was standard to put a suspect in the backseat of a patrol car with his hands cuffed behind him. In some cruisers there was a wire mesh screen that separated the front of the car from the backseat. If an officer became annoyed at a cuffed suspect while transporting him to the station, he'd slam on the brakes, catapulting the man forward, face first against the wire screen. With hands cuffed in back, the suspect could not protect himself. This was referred to as "waffling"—for the screen imprint it left on a suspect's face.

I was personally involved in three situations where I had to use force while I worked for the Grand Rapids PD. Back in those days, you were pretty much out there on your own when you walked a beat. There were no shoulder radios to call for assistance. Instead, there were "call boxes" every few blocks where it was procedure to routinely call in and report your status. You were equipped with a gun, a nightstick, and pair of handcuffs. And your own intelligence and sensibilities to rely on to keep you safe.

I was on patrol in a squad car once when I pulled over a driver who had obviously been drinking. The driver was a man, and with him was a woman. I had the driver get out of the car. I told him he was under arrest. He became belligerent and said he wasn't going to let me take him in. I started to cuff him, but he grabbed me and we both rolled over the hood of his car. I ended up ahold of him as he lay on the ground. He started kicking me. I pulled my club, but he grabbed it and began swinging it at me as I stood over him. I managed to get my blackjack out. Closing my eyes at the thought of it—I hit him hard on the head. He went slack and his head fell back.

His wife started screaming, "You killed Floyd! You killed Floyd!"

Floyd did, in fact, look dead. The wife kept screaming.

I was in shock. I thought I had killed the guy. In great distress, I turned to her. "But I didn't mean to," I pleaded mournfully.

Fortunately for Floyd—and for me—I hadn't killed him. He finally came around and was taken to the hospital and then to jail.

Another incident happened while I walked a beat. I was passing by a jewelry store when a man dashed out, nearly knocking into me, and started sprinting up the sidewalk. The storeowner was fast out the door on his heels and grabbed me by the arm when he saw me.

"That guy just held us up. You gotta stop him," he demanded.

The suspect looked back right at that moment I pulled my gun. I yelled for him to stop. "Or I'll shoot." He kept running. I raised my gun and fired. The guy fell to the ground.

I raced up to where he lay. He was panting furiously. I asked him if he was okay. Was he hit? He said no. I asked him why he fell down. He looked at me sheepishly. "The gunshot scared me." I holstered my weapon and cuffed him, then helped him to his feet.

He drew a breath to collect himself. "Can I ask you something?"

"What?"

"Can I have the casing from the bullet?"

I stared at him in disbelief. "What for?"

"So when I tell my buddies, they'll know I ain't lying."

There was a seminal moment in my time as a police officer in Grand Rapids—an event that stayed with me my whole career in law enforcement, one that deeply affected me. By the time it happened I had gotten over my first-night-on-the-job doubts about being a cop and had settled into the routine of the work. What happened, however, was a powerful object lesson for how insidiously the job can work on you.

I had brought in a drunk I had arrested and was in the process of having him locked up. The "turnkey," the officer who ran the cellblock, was an older black man. I told the drunk to do something, and for some reason, I grew annoyed with how he responded—or perhaps didn't respond. I slapped him hard across the face.

"You better do what I say," I barked. I uncuffed him and placed him in a cell. I was about to leave when the turnkey quietly addressed me.

"Why'd you do that?"

"Excuse me?" I said, taken aback.

"Why did you slap him?" The turnkey's tone was not accusatory, but sadly curious.

"Because he didn't do what I asked him to do," I said.

The turnkey looked at me for a long moment. "That man could be somebody's father." He held my gaze without wavering. "Or somebody's brother. Or uncle." He shook his head. "There's no reason you shoulda done that. He didn't do nothing to you." His tone was understated, matter-of-fact.

He turned and went back to his desk and his paperwork.

I felt awful. Why *had* I done that? What had possessed me to do such a thing?

To my horror, I realized that I'd done it for no other reason than because I could. It's what I'd seen other cops do. Shamed, I had to admit that I'd done it for one simple reason: to be "one of the boys."

It was important to fit in and do well. Though I'd at first been taken aback by the black turnkey's direct outspokenness, he'd provided me an invaluable lesson. At the time, black officers in the department didn't mix with white officers; they were a part of a separate squad. They weren't known for challenging the actions of a white officer. But this gentleman had been affronted by my behavior; no doubt had seen far worse in this day. This time he chose to speak up. And I ultimately was grateful that he had. It made me realize that I needed to follow the rules and regulations, but I also needed to heed my internal compass as to what was right and decent and fair.

CHAPTER THREE

Integrating Changes

Being assigned my own patrol car was a welcome milestone in my advance from rookie to regular officer. It was also satisfying, for I was freer to be more myself dealing with people I encountered during my shift, rather than always taking lead from a more senior patrolman. I'd found that I had a different inclination from many others on the force. Rather than approaching everyone with suspicion and being on guard, I believed that most people you come in contact with are decent, law-abiding citizens.

About the same time that I was assigned my own patrol car, a new superintendent was named to head the Grand Rapids Police Department. He marked a radical point of departure from the past in many ways. Most significantly, soon after taking over, he ended the segregation of whites and blacks on the force, a change I supported.

For years, black officers were assigned to serve exclusively in Squad 88. One of its main functions was to meet arriving trains downtown. All black travelers who disembarked were interrogated by Squad 88 members as to their purpose for coming to the city. If they didn't have a job or family in Grand Rapids, they were told to be on the next train out of town.

In 1958, I was the first white officer to integrate a squad car in the city. By luck of the draw, my new partner was Johnny Stubbs. He was about my age, but he had been on the force maybe a year longer. I liked him from the start. He wasn't a "rock-'em-sock-'em" type. He was funny and fun to be with. We were a lot alike; we both enjoyed noticing the unusual, things that weren't necessarily strictly pre-scribed by the job, but were curiosities or small human dramas we observed while cruising. We'd laugh or comment on it. He had a great sense of humor. We both saw humor in things others might not find funny, but we always found plenty of things that made us appre-ciate the lighter side of life.

When we made traffic stops, I, as the driver, remained in the ve-hicle, and Johnny got out to engage with the other driver. Invariably, he immediately returned to the car. "They want to speak to the white officer," he'd recount. I knew this was a source of deep frustration and humiliation for him. I'd get out and go up to speak to the other driver, but I didn't like it.

This went on for some time. One day early in our shift we stopped a car, and I sat watching as Johnny got out and walked up to the driver's window. I watched as he and the driver exchanged words, and then the driver handed him his license. I observed the ongo-ing interaction with perplexed interest, watching Johnny write out a ticket. He handed it and the license back to the driver and came back and got in our car.

"What happened?" I asked.

"I wrote him up," Johnny said matter-of-factly.

"Yeah?"

He turned to look at me, a big smile lighting his dark face. "I told him I was Hawaiian." And that was that. No more problems.

———

I had been engaged to a girl while I was in the navy, but I received a "Dear John" letter before I got out. After I joined the force, I started dating a young coed, Mary Smith, whom I had met through mutual friends. She was a student at the University of Michigan, studying to be a dental hygienist. She was easy to talk to, and we had a lot in common in terms of values; she was always a champion of the underdog and a strong advocate for social justice. She thought my approach to police work was enlightened. We married in 1958 and settled into a ranch-style house we purchased in a suburban community southwest of the city.

Our daughter Patricia was born in August 1959. I remember sitting in the waiting room, smoking nervously with the other expectant fathers while Mary was in delivery. It was a different time: the delivery room back then was completely off-limits to nervous fathers-to-be. When we settled again at home, Mary gave up her job to take care of the baby because my schedule was totally unpredictable.

I was ambitious and wanted to go back to college, which Mary supported. We borrowed money from her parents and I quit the force in 1960. We moved to East Lansing so I could attend Michigan State University in its police administration program. We were there only a year before Mary became pregnant again. Our daughter Lynn was born in November 1961.

It was abundantly clear that I needed to go back to work in order to support our growing family. I was fortunate to be able to come back to Grand Rapids and rejoin the force. I enrolled at Grand Rapids Community College, the school I'd entered right out of high school, and continued classes there. My superiors were very supportive in assigning me to the afternoon shift and giving me sequential days off during the week so that I could attend classes.

In a sociology class, I sat next to a talkative, friendly guy. He was younger, but we hit it off. He was full of questions about my job as a cop. Due to my full schedule, we never actually hung out together outside of class, but we always chatted as we waited for class to start.

One afternoon while I was on duty, my partner and I responded to a call from the dispatcher to check out an address. A woman had called while she was at work, saying she'd tried to reach her son who was at home, but couldn't. She was concerned. The dispatcher passed along the address and where a spare key was hidden, and we went over to check things out.

We let ourselves in and searched the first and second floors, but didn't find anybody. So we went down to the basement. That was where we found the body. The scene was horrific. It was obvious that the victim had committed suicide: there was an open box of rat poison near the body. The victim's face was greenish and bloated. We left the scene untouched and went back upstairs.

While my partner was calling it in, I wandered through the living room, looking at personal items, wondering what would drive somebody to take his own life. I saw some framed photographs on a piano and went over to view them. In one, I recognized my friend from class. The connection of the ghoulish body in the basement to the good-natured guy in class stunned me. I was near tears when my partner came back into the room to report that the coroner was on the way.

I choked backed my emotions, momentarily shamed by the thought that my partner might see me crying. The ethos that cops didn't show emotions—let alone cry—at a crime scene was deeply ingrained. It was okay to crack sick jokes to release tension, but police officers absolutely did not cry.

I would think about this incident many times over the years and would always find my reaction disturbing. Reacting coldly, aloofly to such a scene is not natural. It may momentarily shield you from the shock and the grief of it, but it's not healthy. Not to the police officer who witnesses it, nor to his circle of family and friends. It hardens the heart, erodes what makes us human. In time, the incident would serve as a powerfully instructive moment, helping me to address what it is about police work that breeds such a response, prompting me to change both my mind-set and my reaction.

I vowed never to forget my friend's death—or my reaction to it. A small thing, perhaps, but it made me a better police officer and, ultimately, a better commander of men who would later serve under me.

My superiors in Grand Rapids were unfailing in their support of my continuing my studies toward a degree in law enforcement. After I finished my course work at the local junior college, they worked out a schedule that enabled me to commute the fifty miles to East Lansing in the afternoons on my days off to again attend classes at MSU. In the fall of 1962, I resigned my position as a police officer and moved to student housing at Michigan State to complete my bachelor's degree.

Toward the end of my last year, I did a two-week internship with the Federal Bureau of Narcotics in Detroit. Though a couple of other students and I were put up in a shabby, rundown hotel at the center of the city, I found the work the agents did intriguing. I didn't get to do any undercover work, but I did get to go out on patrol and had the opportunity to ask countless questions. The agents welcomed my curiosity. My interest was piqued. The Federal Bureau of Narcotics, the forerunner of the Drug Enforcement Agency (DEA), seemed to be the kind of place that offered great challenges in abundance.

CHAPTER FOUR

Embracing Sonny Days

After I graduated in 1963 with a bachelor's of science in police administration, I applied to both the Federal Bureau of Narcotics and the CIA. I loved law enforcement, but I wanted a change from regular police work, and both agencies were focused on activities that I thought were crucial to the health and security of American society. I completed the paperwork—and then waited. I was eager to start as I had a family to support.

The CIA was the first to notify me to come for an interview. I was invited down to its Langley, Virginia, headquarters. I was instructed not to tell anyone where I was going or why. Of course I told my wife, stressing to her, however, that she absolutely could not tell a soul. I traveled to Langley and was put through a rigorous evaluation process, including psychological testing and a polygraph.

During the polygraph test, I was asked if I'd ever stolen anything. "Yes."

"What?"

"A can of Spam."

The questioner looked up from scanning the graph recording and stared incredulously at me. "A can of Spam?"

"I was hungry."

He continued to stare. I told him that in high school, a friend and I worked at a golf course, and one day I'd forgotten my lunch. I didn't have any money so we walked over to a small store and I told my friend to keep the owner distracted. I pocketed the Spam and we left.

The examiner shook his head and went back to asking me the remaining questions on his list. When we finished the main body of questions, he asked a follow-up one.

"You seemed to have had a problem when I asked if you knew anybody in the Communist Party."

I thought for a moment. I told him I didn't personally know anybody, but that I had known *of* someone back in Grand Rapids who had been suspected of being a Communist. To my knowledge, I said, he wasn't.

Before I left Langley, I was told that if I was hired, I would not be able to tell anyone what I did or who I worked for. Officially I would be employed by the US Department of Labor. That would be my cover.

I returned to Michigan, again to wait.

My wife worked as a dental hygienist. While I had been down in Virginia, she had a new client come in for a cleaning. He seemed very interested in me; he asked what I was like, what I was interested in, where I was. It seemed peculiar to her for a stranger to have such keen interest in her husband, which made her suspicious and very circumspect in answering. Apparently the CIA had dispatched someone to find out what my wife knew about my trip to Virginia.

Several weeks passed before I heard from the Federal Bureau of Narcotics. They offered me a job and I took it. Several weeks later, the CIA called to offer me a job. I told them that I'd already accepted a job at the bureau. The CIA officer was extremely upset, saying that the agency had invested a lot of time and money investigating me, doing a thorough background check. (I learned later that they had interviewed friends and people who had known me going back to high school.) I told him I was sorry, but I hadn't heard from them when the bureau called. I accepted its offer because I had a family to support.

I was assigned to the Philadelphia regional office of the Bureau of Narcotics. I found an apartment to rent in Upper Darby, a suburb west of the city, and started work in July 1963. The regional office was housed in the old federal Customs House downtown and had a handful of agents responsible for covering half of Pennsylvania and New Jersey, including Atlantic City and Trenton, and all of Delaware. Philadelphia was its major area of concentration. Samuel Levine was the supervisor in charge. He was a career agent who'd come up through the ranks. He was in his late forties, very steady, reserved, and understated. He expected you to do your job, but strongly supported his team.

Sunday evening the first week on the job, the phone at home rang. It was a detective with the Camden, New Jersey, Police Department, just across the river from downtown Philadelphia. He said that he had information from an informant about a guy who wanted to sell a half pound of pure heroin.

"Okay."

"I need someone at the bureau to make the buy."

"Okay?" I answered cautiously.

"You're on call, right?"

"What do you mean?"

"You're the agent covering the weekend."

"Yeah."

"Well, I need you to make the buy."

"*Me?*"

"Yeah. I need you to come over here so we can plan out how it's going to go down."

Nobody in the bureau had mentioned anything about working with any area police departments as an undercover agent. I hadn't even been to the bureau training academy yet.

"I'm kinda new," I said.

"That's okay. Come on over and we'll walk you through it."

"Ah, can you tell me how to get there?"

Undercover work? What the hell did I know about undercover work? I called the bureau agent I'd been assigned to for orientation but he wasn't home. So I got in the car and drove over to meet the detective and his informant.

Purportedly, the seller was representing a friend who'd obtained the heroin from a seaman from Spain who'd jumped ship in Camden. On the ride with the informant down to Gloucester, a suburban community south of Camden, I acted like I knew what I was doing, but I was nervous as hell. We'd made a plan, but it left a lot to the imagination—and to my ability to be inventive on the fly. I decided I'd play a no-nonsense tough guy, a guy with "attitude."

It was disconcerting that the seller wasn't out on the street where he'd said he'd be. The informant directed me to cruise farther down and turn onto a cross street. The informant saw the seller walking along the sidewalk and we pulled over.

The seller was in his mid-thirties, of average height and weight, with dark hair. The informant introduced us and then got out of the car so the seller could get in and we could conduct the deal.

I jumped right to it. "Whadda ya got?"

"About half a pound of heroin."

"You got it widcha?"

He nodded. He pulled an instant coffee-sized jar wrapped in a white handkerchief out of his coat pocket. It was nearly full of an off-white powder.

"Where you from?" he asked.

"New York. Where the *fuck* you from!?" I made it clear this wasn't a social meet and greet. I eyed the jar and gave a nod.

"I ain't gonna do nothin' tonight," I said. "I gotta make sure you're not puttin' me on."

"This is good shit."

"I'll tell *you* if it's good shit. I'm gonna take a nickel. If it's good shit, we do it."

I took a pack of cigarettes out of my pocket and emptied it of smokes, then had him put a small amount of the white powder in the packet. I folded it up and put it in my pocket. I gave him a number at the Philadelphia bureau office that we used only for buys.

"Call me ta-morrow at noon and I'll tell ya if it's gonna happen."

Monday morning, Sam Levine casually asked how the weekend went.

"I got this stuff over the weekend."

"What do you mean?"

"Heroin."

Levine's eyes went wide. "You did what?"

"A detective from the Camden PD called me and said he needed me to make an undercover buy. So I did. We tested it. It's heroin."

Levine was incredulous. "Do you know what you've done?"

"No," I said.

"My god. How did you do it?"

"I don't know. I just talked funny."

"You haven't even been here a week," Levine said, beside himself with amazement.

"I did the best I could," I offered. I told him the guy was supposed to call at noon to see if I wanted to make the buy.

At noon, the phone rang and we arranged to meet at four o'clock in a parking lot near where we'd been the night before. Levine immediately dispatched a couple of agents to head over to do surveillance before I got there.

I drove over and arrived on time, but nobody was there to meet me. After a bit, I noticed a laundry truck driving back and forth through the shopping center lot. Finally it cruised over to where I was parked. I sat and watched the guy I'd met the night before get out and come over to the car. I told him to get in. I knew I was being surveilled somewhere by the two agents from the office. We'd agreed that they were to move in for the bust when they saw me get out of the car and light a cigarette.

I put on my New Yorker attitude. "You got the stuff?" I said. No smile. No bullshit. All business.

"Yeah. You got the money?"

"Yeah. It's in the trunk." There wasn't anything in the trunk but the spare tire. "Let me see the stuff first."

I took the jar, inspected it. I handed it back.

I got out on my side and he got out on the other. I pulled my pack of cigarettes out and lit one. I made a big deal blowing a plume of smoke into the air.

Nothing. Nobody came.

I took another hit, exhaled, growing more nervous by the second. I took a quick hit and coughed, pretending to struggle to catch my breath.

The seller was clearly agitated.

"You gonna buy or what?"

I took another drag, letting my eyes slowly scan the area as if I was making sure it was safe to buy. I noticed the surveillance vehicle rolling toward us at a good clip. *About fucking time.*

I dropped my cigarette and crushed it under my foot.

"Oh yeah."

The surveillance vehicle stopped abruptly and the two agents leaped out, guns drawn, one agent keeping an eye on the driver in the laundry truck, the other coming toward the seller and me.

"Federal Bureau of Narcotics. You're under arrest."

Despite my nerves, it was an easy pinch. The pair was just a couple of guys who thought they would make some quick money selling a little junk. Instead of spending money, they ended up with time in a federal penitentiary. We nailed them, got the dope, and confiscated the laundry truck, which the bureau put to good use on numerous occasions doing surveillances over the next several years.

The weekend bust boosted my reputation around the office for being savvy at undercover work. It also earned me an award from the Federal Bureau of Narcotics commissioner. It set the course for my career at the bureau, something I took pride in and seemed to have a natural talent for: being an undercover narc.

My new cover? I was a South Philly pimp buying drugs for his girls. Everyone in the office—including me—knew it would be a challenge from the get-go. The heroin trade in Philadelphia was almost entirely controlled by black dealers. Only black agents had ever been used to do undercover work before—and even then, not to any great success.

But I loved the challenge. Challenges—or people telling me I can't do something—always spurred me to try harder. I was all in. I bought a gold pinky ring with fake inset diamond and two rubies and was given a blue 1961 Buick convertible, a vehicle the bureau had confiscated elsewhere during a bust. I assumed the persona of William "Sonny" Sonetti, a poker-faced pimp with a "stingy brim" hat—a street style of the day—who flashed cash and a Zippo lighter with "Sonny" engraved on the side.

My "Sonny days" had officially commenced.

The big unanswered question, however, was how well the big Buick convertible, my bad attitude, and my white Irish face were going to play as an Italian pimp on the streets of South Philly.

CHAPTER FIVE

Glimpses of the Dark Side

In the haze of summer, downtown Philadelphia rose like a sharp, jagged upthrust of towering buildings clustered along a sweep of the Delaware River. Radiating outward around it were smaller business areas and neighborhoods, each with its own character and history. South Philly was a sprawling patchwork of two-story row houses and old brick warehouses that stretched from South Street on the periphery of downtown down to where the Delaware River on the east made a sharp westward turn. The Schuylkill River bounded it on the west. This area officially joined the city in the mid-1800s when growth driven by the immigration of first Irish, then Italians and Poles, coming for jobs in the countless small manufacturing concerns that made South Philly a working-class haven. Blacks began to flow out of the Deep South and settle in South Philly in the early twentieth century, seeking to escape the repression of Jim Crow and gain greater employment opportunity. By the late 1950s and early 1960s, the manufacturing base began to relocate, elevating unemployment and crime, particularly in the most southern area, while other areas and neighborhoods continued to prosper. The heroin trade was relegated to the seedier pockets in the black section of South Philly. This became the native habitat for Sonny Sonetti, my undercover alter ego.

I would kiss my family good-bye in modest Upper Darby and commute to South Philly, a distance of only a dozen miles or so, but a journey that put light years between me and all that was safe and familiar. As Sonny Sonetti, I spent much of my time cruising the streets, making my presence known. It wasn't hard, as I was one of the only white faces to be seen. In the early going, I always had someone known in the area riding with me, a black offender who we'd secretly turned to become one of our informants. Even still, I would get sharp stares when we pulled over to chat with someone he knew, asking if they were "doing anything." Together, we'd go into local bars and taverns where he knew people, and he'd introduce me around. My cover was that I had a string of prostitutes for whom I bought heroin and other drugs. I flashed cash. Eventually I made my first buy. Then I made another. Word got around that I was okay to do business with. My white face still stood out, but when I cruised in my big shiny Buick, I'd get nods and a finger wave in response to an arched-eyebrow inquiry if anything was available.

My job was to deeply infiltrate the South Philly heroin network, one link at a time. It required that I often worked the junkies. I'd give them a lift out of the neighborhood to a distant shopping area where nobody knew them, and let them out to do their shoplifting to get merchandise they could fence to buy another fix. It was all a part of what I had to do to get to the next level, make the next introduction, following the flow higher toward the source.

It required patience and persistence. But in time, it got to where some of my connections would call out to me from the sidewalk, seeing me cruise by. "Hey, Sonny. You looking?" I was always good for business. My incessant success was a marvel to Sam Levine and the other agents downtown. The Philadelphia bureau had never before had a white agent working South Philly. They all thought it was an impossible proposition. For some reason, I was good at it.

I was always buying for my phantom prostitutes. I never played an addict. If I'd gone the addict route, I'd have been expected to shoot up. I grew pretty comfortable in my role as Sonny Sonetti. I was never especially concerned that they might think I was a cop. If they thought I was a cop, they'd simply stop doing business with me. The much graver risk was that they might suspect that I was an informant. To be fingered as an informant could be a death sentence.

Whenever I found myself in encounters where anyone got hinky and questioned me, I'd jump hard in their faces. "*Hey!* You working with the fuckin' cops? You better not be. You lie to me, I find out—you're going down. I promise ya!" That usually ended the discussion.

Slowly, steadily, I moved up the food chain. I had my eye set on a major dealer by the name of Mumford. He had a menacing presence, someone not to be screwed with. For the longest time, he wouldn't have anything to do with me. He didn't trust white guys. But eventually I won him over. We got to be fairly familiar with one another over time. He may not have liked white guys, but I *intensely* disliked him. I'd cruise the neighborhood where he hung out and pull over whenever I saw him. I'd ask him if he had anything; he'd ask how much I wanted. We'd make the deal and then he'd disappear. I always stayed in the car.

Five or ten minutes later I'd see his five-year-old daughter come sauntering up the cracked and broken sidewalk. She'd be all pretty and smiling, swinging a little purse on her arm. I'd grit my teeth in disgust at Mumford, but smile at her as she approached me.

"Hi, Sonny," she'd beam.

"Hey, sweetie."

She'd open her purse and extend a bag to me. "My daddy told me to give this to you."

I'd smile and thank her and watch her turn and walk back down the street and around the corner.

The bureau began to set up a big bust, working to arrest ten different dealers, including Mumford. I worked weeks to put it together in conjunction with other agents doing surveillance. Finally, we did a coordinated sweep and picked up nine of the ten dealers we'd targeted. All but Mumford. He had disappeared.

It was big news that we had cracked a major heroin ring. Everybody in the city administration and the bureau was ecstatic. A news article was headlined "Nine Arrested—Police Used Spy."

"The undercover agent was often in danger in the world of heroin," the news story read. "Several peddlers once became suspicious and ordered him to use narcotics in their presence, the police said. He managed through a ruse to dispose of the drugs." Another clip stated that the undercover agent had spent "countless hours of overtime and whose initiative and ingenuity played an important part." High praise, certainly, but I was still gravely disappointed that we had hadn't nailed Mumford and taken him off the streets.

I kept my ear out for where he'd gone. The word was that he was lying low in New York City. Though we put out a fugitive arrest warrant, nothing came of it.

I continued to go about my business. A few days after the bust I was out cruising a new section of South Philly when one of the junkies I knew flagged me over, all excited to tell me about the bust. "Some white guy buying dope was behind it." He went on to describe the "snitch" to me—describing me in great detail in the process. I nodded. He warned me to be careful. I told him I would and thanked him for the tip.

Several weeks later I was out when I saw Mumford walking down the street. I was surprised to see him. I pulled over next to him.

"Hey Mumf. Haven't seen ya around. Whatcha doin'?" He said he was going home. I told him to hop in, that I'd give him a lift. We made small talk; I asked him how he'd been, all the while keeping my eye out for a Philadelphia squad car. Funny how when you need a cop, you can never find one. I kept a small .32 automatic under the seat. I ended up cruising past the street to his house.

"Where you going?" he demanded. "You shoulda turned." I didn't say anything. "Pull over," he threatened. "I'm gettin' out."

I slowed and drifted toward the curb. I pulled the gun from under the seat and aimed it point-blank at him. "No. You're not."

His face turned into a mask of outrage.

"What the…?"

"You're under arrest. You try to get out, I'm gonna shoot you."

He started at me incredulous. I spotted a squad car and flagged him over. I was never as joyous in my job as I was at that moment. Mumford was finally going down.

A report on the bust was sent to Henry L. Giordano, the national commissioner of the Federal Bureau of Narcotics. The report read in part, "Heroin and marijuana continue to be the main drugs in the traffic. Marijuana is in plentiful supply but heroin is in short supply. Information received from informants indicate that addicts are having a difficult time obtaining heroin during the past several weeks."

There was a section on Mumford: "In investigations in South Philadelphia area, undercover agent learned James was one of the major suppliers buying in New York City…Undercover agent met him…[and] made three purchases. Others arrested. James fled. Weeks later undercover agent saw him, asked him into his car and arrested him."

For this work, Daniel Addario, another agent who worked closely with me, and I received a Superior Performance Award from Commissioner Giordano. The submitted report for the award stated, "Almost exclusively during the past several years the cases developed in this District have been against Negro traffickers. In the development of those cases it has required the use of Negro undercover agents and officers from the Philadelphia Police Department. Previous efforts to persuade potential informants to introduce agents of Caucasian descent to their Negro sources of supply have uniformly met with resistance which amounted to a statement of policy that these traffickers did not and would not deal with other than Negroes."

Sam Levine, my boss who submitted the report, went on to describe my lead in the bust: "These cases developed in this series are outstanding in light of the problems inherent in a white agent dealing with Negro violators…in an area exclusively Negro, who also never deal with other than Negro customers and then only if they know Negro customers over a long period of time."

It was deeply satisfying to get the citation award and a check for $200. But greater still was my satisfaction in seeing Mumford sentenced to a long stretch in the federal pen.

CHAPTER SIX

Through the Looking Glass—A Foot in Both Worlds

In the underworld of heroin trafficking, everybody went by nicknames. Nobody ever talked about anything personal—family, your life story, where you lived. Whenever anybody I encountered edged across that boundary, I pushed back hard. "Who the fuck are you? You a snitch or somethin'?" That ended the discussion, as nobody wanted to be challenged as a snitch. It wasn't good for your health.

There was a bar in South Philly where a lot of action took place that I wanted to get in on. The bureau hadn't been able to penetrate it before, even with a black undercover agent. So I had a mug shot made, supposedly processed by the Wilmington, Delaware, police following an arrest. It showed me in a white striped shirt, collar open, sporting a crew cut. I wore a stark, blank stare, almost a glower. There was an understated menace in my eyes.

I had a couple of Philadelphia detectives take it into the bar one night and flash it around, asking if anybody had seen me. Nobody had. But even if they had, nobody would have said anything. Someone asked why they were looking for me. They got a simple, evasive answer: "We want to talk to him." The implication was clear: I was into something that had the cops out looking for me.

A week later I went into the bar acting like a regular: no hesitancy, no fear. Immediately I got word that the cops had been in asking about me.

"Motha-*fucker*!" I snarled. I ordered a drink and was soon engaged in conversations with several players involved in drug trafficking in the area.

One of my great strengths as an undercover narc was my talent for thinking up ways to establish unquestionable bona fides among those with nefarious dealings on the dark side of the law. I aggressively cultivated my persona as Sonny Sonetti, the fearless white pimp. The guy who went where he wanted, when he wanted, and talked to whomever he wanted. I didn't let it go to my head, and I never allowed myself to be careless. I had a horrifically challenging job to do, and I took great pleasure in doing it well. But nevertheless, it was important to always be alert. Gaining access to this South Philly bar—more accurately being "welcomed" there—resulted in eventually upending the career paths of numerous of its patrons.

It was just one of the places to which I was able to gain access. I sometimes frequented "shooting galleries," typically filthy rooms off back alleys or in seedy buildings where junkies shot up. These galleries and its denizens were not pretty sights, for most regular visitors were the worst of the worst junkies, often little more than specters of their former selves. Shooting galleries provided patrons with a guaranteed service: no matter now physically deteriorated you were, the dealers who ran them ensured that they'd help you find a vein to tap. I remember being in one gallery one night when I encountered a junkie I knew, an older woman who was all tied off ready to shoot up. She'd been injecting for so long that all the veins in her arms were collapsed. She turned to me with a wasted, desperate expression. "Sonny, gimme a hand. Squeeze my arm for me, wouldcha?"

The world I inhabited was very strange, in large ways and small. A world most people can't even begin to image. It had extremely dark corners and twisted realities—like fathers who'd send their five-year-old daughters out to deliver heroin. Much of it was like looking through radically warped glass—features of its inhabitants and the landscape resembled elements in the real world, but they were grotesquely distorted. I vividly remember the day that President Kennedy was assassinated. I was driving down the Delaware Expressway with an informant to Chester, Pennsylvania, when the music we were listening to on the radio was interrupted with news of Kennedy being shot. I was stunned speechless. I hung on every word that the newscaster spoke. The informant, a former small-time dealer, and I rode along in silence for a couple of miles, listening to the grave report. And then the informant grew irritated. "Christ. What's the big deal? Put some music on, why don'tcha?"

I glanced at him. "The president's been shot," I stammered.

"Yeah. So? Let's listen to some music."

In addition to constantly guarding against becoming overconfident, you also had to guard against allowing the job to become toxically corrosive. Heroin is a scourge. It steals souls and turns lives into wastelands, and sooner or later—more often than not—it kills. The roots of addiction go exceedingly deep, and pushers feeding the addiction take advantage of the ills of society that fracture the lives of uncountable individuals, disproportionately those in the great underclass of poverty and foreclosed dreams.

I was good at what I did, and took pride in doing it. I saw my job as severing the supply lines that insidiously snaked their way into the most vulnerable parts of the community.

I was at the same time a member of privileged society, with a family living in safe and secure Upper Darby. My two daughters, Pat and Lynn, grew from toddlers to preschoolers. My wife, Mary, was an attentive mother, making sure that their lives were as normal as possible under the circumstances. I worked long days, long nights, and weekends. I knew little of the normalcy that my family knew. Though I continued to maintain the inner identity of William McClaran, for all intents and purposes I passed through the world as Sonny Sonetti, the dope-buying pimp in the big blue Buick. People on the streets in the shadier side of South Philly would call out to me as I passed, "Hey, Sonny! You looking?" I was a good, regular, dependable customer. If somebody was selling, I was buying. Often while my wife and two young daughters were home asleep in their beds.

I had a foot in both worlds on either side of that warped glass, worlds that were nearly inscrutable from one to the other. Whether I liked it or not, I spent almost all of my time on the dark side of the looking glass. South Philly was more home to me than Upper Darby in terms of the streets I traveled and the people I shared my life with. It was a strange existence, indeed, that I inhabited.

CHAPTER SEVEN

Stepping Off in Detroit

And then suddenly, I was pulled out of Philadelphia after eighteen months and transferred to Detroit at the end of 1964. Just like that.

It was standard procedure in the Federal Bureau of Narcotics to move agents frequently as sooner or later—and typically sooner for undercover agents—the balance tipped dangerously toward diminishing returns. The bureau always wanted to move an agent in advance of that tipping point. It didn't matter whether your kids were in the middle of a school term, or you'd just bought a house, or any other of the myriad tendrils of a normal life you might be attempting to sink down in the community where you and your family lived. It was much like the military: the bureau came first. It's what you'd signed on for.

We moved and rented a house in a neighborhood in a suburb west of downtown Detroit. Mary settled the family while I reported to work. The first day on the job I met Ross Ellis, supervisor of the Detroit region. Ellis had a reputation for being very fair with the agents on his team. But the first thing he said when I stepped into his office took me aback.

"What kind of trouble did you get in?"

"I didn't get in any trouble," I said.

"They always send me the screw-ups—those that need straightening out," he replied, looking me over. "Let me make myself clear. I run a tight ship here. I expect you to do your job—and do it well. And your job is putting bad guys in jail."

"Yes, sir."

The Detroit office was staffed similarly to the Philadelphia office. There were six to eight agents that covered a broad, multistate area. We covered Detroit and all of Michigan and Indiana. We also covered parts of Ohio and Canada. I was the only undercover agent in the region.

After I'd been on the job a couple of days, Ellis called me back in his office. "I'm sorry for suggesting you were some kind of malcontent. I checked you out. Heard a lot of good things about your work in Philadelphia. I'm glad you're here."

"Glad to be here," I said.

End of discussion. I was confident I had his backing.

The work schedule was the same as before. I put in seventy- and eighty-hour weeks, working days, nights, and weekends. I rarely saw my kids—they were in bed when I came home and I was gone before they got up. When I was around, I was always preoccupied with work: scheming how to play a meeting with a new dealer; calculating how to work my way into a new situation; wondering if I could trust an informant. Whenever I was actually at home, from my family's perspective it was like nobody was "home" inside of me. I was devoted to the job—and I was ambitious. Detroit was a whole new challenge.

———

One of our key tasks as federal agents involved months of investigation and legwork to make a case leading to an arrest. Another major task was then spending weeks to flip those we had a solid case on, bringing them over to our side as an informant. Leniency in sentencing was always the carrot dangled to entice them to cooperate. The objective was to climb the food chain ever higher in order to nail the big players. Still, it was always weird to me: working endless hours to bust someone and then turning around and soliciting favors from him or her. But it was part of the job.

I had been in Detroit only a few weeks when I was called back to Philadelphia to testify in a case I'd worked there. While down in Philly, I made contact with one of the informants working with the Detroit office. I instructed him to arrange to pick me up at the airport when I returned, but to be sure to bring along a couple of street dealers so that they could see me getting off the plane from Philly. The informant was to tell them that I was coming to Detroit to meet some people.

The day I returned, I was greeted by the informant, who was white, and two black street peddlers he'd brought to the airport with him. I was dressed as always in chinos, a dress shirt open at the collar, and my trademark "stingy-brim" hat. Introductions were made. We rode back into Detroit making small talk about my trip to Philly. I mentioned to them that I had been in Detroit a little more than a year and was running a string of girls who were always in need of shit.

Later, we were together on the street in a black neighborhood close to downtown when we ran into one of the two street dealers' main sources. The two I'd met earlier introduced me to "Rocky." They related how they'd picked me up at the airport, coming in from Philly. We all chatted, with me laying out my story and relating that

I was always looking for a reliable supply. I could tell their guy was assessing me. I was feeling good that it was a good first meeting.

I happened to run into Rocky alone on the street the next day. We were cautiously friendly—and then he surprised me.

"Why don't you and I go back to my place?" he said.

I shrugged. "Sure. Why not?"

Rocky lived only a couple blocks away. We strolled leisurely along, with him pointing out points of interest, good places to eat, small shops where one could always get a deal, and merchants to stay away from. I followed him upstairs to his second-floor apartment. The apartment wasn't fancy, but it was decent and neat. He indicated I should take a chair in front of a low table as he sat down on a couch opposite. I was thinking that this was working out a whole lot faster than I had expected. We sat facing one another for a moment. Then he leaned forward and opened a small drawer in the table and pulled out a gun. He laid it on the tabletop in front of him.

I didn't avert my eyes from the intense scrutiny he was paying me. We sat in silence, a vast enveloping hush that drowned out all street noise outside. The mood in the room and my mental frame shifted dramatically. It was like someone had just shoved me off of a cliff and I was falling in slow motion.

This fucking doesn't look good.

I mustered every ounce of Sonny Sonetti at my disposal. I fixed him coldly with a calculating stare of my own.

"That make you feel better, does it?" I said evenly. I showed no emotion, no surprise, no fear.

Rocky sat leaning forward with his forearms resting on his knees. I was peripherally aware of his long slender fingers dangling down, moving loosely, ever so slightly. He drew a breath, straightening, but didn't lean back into the cushions. The gun remained within easy reach. I knew it to be a sub-nosed Colt .38. Not big, but extremely lethal, especially at close range. It was a favorite among undercover cops and bad guys alike because of its power and compact size, making it easy to carry concealed. I was unarmed.

"You say you know Philly," he said.

I didn't respond.

"Well, I know Philly," he said, a wry smile now lighting his dark face. "Let's you and me talk Philly."

"All right. Let's talk Philly."

He started asking me questions about people and places. I knew a few of the people he mentioned, and I recounted stories about them. He asked me about various restaurants and bars on such-and-such streets. I knew South Philly and casually corrected him when he tried to subtly trip me up by making up some place that didn't exist, or a place he located on the wrong street. I could see him begin to relax.

I began asking him questions about South Philly, in part to test the depth of his knowledge, but also to ferret out any possible danger points where I'd have to be careful about what I said. I also fabricated bars and juke joints where drugs deals were consummated.

"You ever been into Pinochle's on South Broad?" I asked, warming to our reminiscing. No such place existed.

"Oh yeah. Couple times. But it ain't my favorite place," he said.

I bet not, I thought. "Ain't bad, but there's better rib joints," I said.

After nearly an hour, I asked him if he knew anybody. "You know, here in Detroit." He understood exactly what I meant: I was looking to buy.

"I know some people," he said.

"I'd like to meet 'em. I'm running some girls here. They're always wantin' shit," I said smiling, shaking my head.

"The bitches are like that."

"Oh yeah. But I gotta keep 'em happy, know what I mean."

"Yeah," he smiled. "I know whatcha mean."

I looked at my watch and told him I needed to go. I had people to meet. "I'll catch up widcha later."

"I'll talk to a couple guys I know."

I nodded. "Appreciate it."

He walked me to the door. "See ya 'round," I said.

"Yeah. See ya 'round. Gimme me a couple days."

South Philly? Yeah, I knew South Philly—a whole lot better than Rocky did. And our little exchange made me feel confident about a door opening before me, giving me the opportunity to get to know Detroit.

I bought several times from Rocky in the weeks ahead, and he introduced me to several other players who were trafficking. I was off to a good start. Meeting him led to several important cases and arrests within a matter of months after my coming to town.

I clearly knew Philly. And now through Rocky, I was definitely getting to know the lay of Detroit and who the players were. And Rocky never suspected that I was anyone but who I said I was: Sonny Sonetti, a dour-faced pimp with a stable of whores who loved their smack.

CHAPTER EIGHT

Wild and Wily

Major dealers who'd been in business a long time and who had learned the hard way—getting busted and doing time—were very circumspect about encounters with anyone new. It was like going to the joint caused many of them to morph into a new breed of animal. Those who successfully went back into the business had highly attuned street smarts and a keen sense for reading people. They also sought to always maintain several degrees of separation from anything that could tie them to a deal. And they never made stupid, careless mistakes. Or almost never. You had to be patient and alert, adaptive and clever—and lucky—to catch a break and penetrate their fortress mentality.

Through an informant, I managed to meet a street dealer who worked for one of the biggest pushers in Detroit. People on the street knew him only as Hersh. He had done a long stretch of time in prison, time during which he no doubt rehashed every move of every deal that had cascaded into him being busted and put away. Despite the hard time he'd done, it was only a short period after he was released before we surmised that he was back into heroin trafficking in Detroit. It spoke legions about his self-confidence. I wanted badly to nail him.

But I couldn't figure out how to get close to him. He maintained a sterile remove from directly handling any dope transactions, whether marijuana or heroin. Finally I hit upon a scheme that I thought had merit and was worth trying. I decided I would approach him sideways.

I started with a street dealer we suspected was tied to his operations. He and Hersh lived in the same large apartment building. I knew the street dealer as Charlie; he was one of the regular peddlers that I bought from. Making a buy one day, I mentioned to Charlie that I had something I thought his boss might be interested in. He asked what it was. I laid out the scam and asked if he'd give me his boss's phone number. I expected him to turn me down. I imagined it would take a long courtship to get it out of him. I was shocked when he gave me the number without question. He thought the scheme was indeed something that Hersh would be interested in.

I called Hersh on a Sunday evening. It was surprising to me how so many bad guys succumbed to magical thinking, believing that cops didn't work on Sundays. Many of them let their guards down on Sunday—if only a bit. Time and again, Sundays had been golden for me. It was one of the reasons that I almost always worked weekends. I was counting on my calling on Sunday catching him off guard, enough so to gain access.

"Who's this?" Hersh demanded when he picked up the phone at home.

"This is Sonny. You don't know me, but I've been working with Charlie. I happened to mention that I had this source for phony twenties."

"Yeah? So?" He was definitely interested.

"They're beautiful. You can't tell they're dirty. No way. Charlie told me I should call you, that you might be interested."

"Yeah? How'd you get 'em?"

I told him I had a friend downstate. That I was helping him unload them. Hersh was silent for a bit, then gave me his address and told me to come by.

I had a crisp, spanking new twenty-dollar bill just off the press at Treasury tucked into my shirt pocket. When I got up to his apartment, we managed our way through quick pleasantries, and then he wanted to see it.

"I only got one," I said, lifting it out of my pocket, snapping it between pinched fingers. "But it's a beaut." I handed it to him.

He took it over to a light and artfully inspected it. "Fucking *beautiful*," he whispered, turning it side to side, eyeing it from several angles.

"Yeah. Ain't it? You interested?"

"How many you got?" he asked, turning to me, continuing to rub the bill between his fingers.

"How many you want? My guy downstate has a shitload. All just like the one in your hand. You give me an order, and I'll get 'em for ya. Take me a week, maybe ten days to deliver 'em."

He studied me. I don't imagine he'd had many white guys standing in his living room. He didn't know me from nobody. I could tell he was dying to do the deal. But he was wary. He was beyond wary. It totally went against his instincts.

He shook his head. "I don't know." He was lasering me to detect any unease, any sign of a "tell" that would give me away.

I didn't flinch. "It ain't like the supply's unlimited," I said nonchalantly. "Charlie said you might be interested. He's always been straight with me, so I thought I'd give you a shot at 'em."

I saw the mask of intense suspicion soften a smudge. "Let me think 'bout it."

"Let me know," I said. "But don't think too long." I extended my hand and waited. He lifted the bill for a final inspection, a tight grimace recasting his face. He lifted his eyes to appraise me one final time and then handed the bill back. I folded it once and slipped it into my shirt pocket.

"Find out how much it'll cost me to get a thousand of 'em."

I nodded. "I'll get back to you."

I called him the next Sunday and told him I'd talked with my guy. "When can we meet?" Again he invited me to come by. I laid the deal out. It was one he couldn't refuse. He said he was in. I said I'd have his order in a week. It was obvious that Hersh was excited and eager to get his hands on a new stream of revenue.

"Say—is Charlie around?" I asked casually as I was about to leave.

"Don't know."

"I was hoping I could 'do somethin'.'"

He left me in his apartment and went off somewhere else in the building. Several minutes later, Charlie came into the room and asked if I wanted to "do somethin'." I told him I wanted five bags. Charlie and I completed our little side deal and I departed.

I called a couple days later to tell Hersh I'd been lucky and had secured his order ahead of schedule. He invited me over. I went, only this time I went with backup. When Hersh opened the door, I had my badge and my gun out.

He stared in shock. He'd been so blinded by greed thinking about turning a big stack of counterfeit twenties that he never paused to consider the risk in going to get Charlie for me. I told him he was under arrest for accessory to dealing drugs.

"You son of a bitch," he seethed.

I watched as my backup cuffed him and led him down the hall in front of me. Hersh was looking at a very long stay in the pen. He'd no doubt have a lot of time to rehash again the foibles of greed while he was sitting in prison—safely removed by leagues of separation from being connected to any deals.

———

I met all kinds as an undercover narc. Though many were absolute lowlifes leading pitiful lives, some were quite charming. A few I even liked. One guy had me home for dinner to meet his family. Some were clearly very intelligent and sophisticated.

I met one guy through an informant who had an elaborate scam selling prescription drugs. He was college educated and lived in a nice house outside Detroit. Nothing about him would catch your eye and make you suspicious if you encountered him on the streets.

Back in those days, it wasn't difficult to get your hands on doctors' prescription pads. You could find them lying around most doctors' offices. They weren't carefully guarded as they are now. This guy had a stack of them, and he had a whole network of young runners he dispatched to pharmacies all over the area to pick up prescriptions he'd phone in. He'd always tell the pharmacist that he had a bedridden patient that needed pain meds immediately. He'd engage the pharmacist using highly technical medical and pharmaceutical terms with complete ease and accuracy.

The routine involved always having one of his runners in the store waiting to overhear the call when it came in. If the scout observed any sign of suspicion on the part of a pharmacist, or if the call didn't go smoothly, the runner would go find a pay phone and report back to nix the deal. If everything did go smoothly, another runner pretending to be the patient's son would show up with the prescription in hand to pick up the drugs.

I ended up meeting the drug scammer through an informant, and I was invited out to his house on several occasions to buy out of his "pharmacy." One afternoon we were out together riding in my car. He loved to talk—about everything and anything. He was widely read and extremely bright. We were in the middle of a conversation as we rode along when he suddenly went quiet.

"You know what I'd like to do?" he said wistfully after a bit.

"What's that?"

"I'd like to kill somebody."

I glanced over and could see that he was dead serious.

"Why you want to do that?" I asked.

"I've always wanted to know what it felt like."

I took a deep breath, taking this in. "Who would you kill?"

"Some nobody. Some homeless person. Somebody that wouldn't be missed."

It didn't take much probing to learn that he possessed a gun and that he was just waiting for the right time and the right person to come along.

There was no question that he needed to be taken down immediately.

I called the next day to tell him that my cousin was in town, just passing through, and that he wanted to buy some drugs before leaving. "Dr. Strangelove" told me to bring him by.

So I and another agent drove out to his house. He greeted us warmly and let us in. Once we were inside, I flashed my badge.

"You're under arrest."

Without a moment's hesitation, he snatched the badge out of my hand. He inspected it in a glance, held it up, and shook it in in my face.

"Do you *know* what we can *do* with this?" he said excitedly. His imagination was roaring like it was on steroids.

"Gimme my damn badge back!" I demanded, grabbing it away from him. "I said you're under *arrest*."

He looked at me like I had two heads, clearly struggling to make sense of the moment. It was like he was rapid shuffling a deck of cards, trying to find the one that could decipher what "arrest" meant. My being an undercover narc hadn't entered his universe. To him, scamming prescription drugs and scheming to kill somebody were everyday ordinary behaviors.

His perplexity shifted slowly to an expression of disappointment. Whatever he'd imagined being able to do with my badge dissolved finally into understanding: there was, indeed, a universe where he didn't control everything. We cuffed him and drove him downtown to book him.

CHAPTER NINE

Unexpected Scariest Moment

I worked leads that led me all over Michigan and into Indiana and Canada. Unlike local cops who were happy to opportunistically bust low-level buyers on a moment's notice, I typically worked months to infiltrate operations as high up as I could go.

I always carried a "Michigan bankroll"—a roll of bills with big denominations wrapping the outside. I'd flash it to let people know I was ready to do business, but had to be careful, too, that I wasn't being set up to be robbed.

I did marijuana buys that led to arrests down in South Bend and up in Flint. When we were ready to bust the ring in Flint, Ross Ellis, my boss, said he wanted to ride along to see how it went down. It was unusual to have the regional supervisor out on an undercover bust, but it was fine all the same with me. Our surveillance team coordinated with local and state authorities, and when I did the next buy, we were able to arrest the five who ran the operation. Ellis was quoted in the local newspaper saying it had required "six to eight weeks of surveillance during which time the undercover agent purchased quantities of marijuana."

The article also identified the undercover agent who worked the case as "known only as Sonny." I was none too happy. There was no way that bit of information came from anyone on the bureau's team.

We never learned where it came from, but most likely it was let slip by one of the local officers involved in the bust. It kept me on edge for weeks, but fortunately it didn't have any repercussions in Detroit or in any of the heroin cases I was actively working.

Some while later, it happened that Mary, my wife, and I were in Grand Rapids visiting family, and there was an opportunity for me to meet with a heroin dealer that I'd recently been introduced to there. Mary and I had left the family car at home in Detroit and had taken the white '62 Cadillac convertible that was a part of my Sonny persona. It was long and sleek and an aerodynamic beauty that featured flared tailfins that made it look like a missile. The night I went out to meet the guy and make the buy at a park, I asked my wife to go along with me. She'd done this once before, playing the role of one of my "girls."

Soon after we parked where we'd agreed to meet, the seller, a clean-cut young guy who could've passed for a kid in college, came over and got in the backseat. We made a small talk for a bit. He was personable and engaging; he seemed like an ordinary young person, someone with his whole life ahead of him.

At one point my wife started to turn to say something to him.

"Shut the fuck up!" I snapped. Without a word, my wife turned back to stare out the windshield.

We negotiated the buy and he got out to go get the stuff. While we were sitting there, Mary asked in a concerned tone what would happen to the young man. I told her that he'd probably get sentenced to ten years in the federal pen.

"But he's so *nice*," she complained.

"Yeah. He is," I replied. "But he's also a heroin dealer."

We sat waiting in a heavy silence.

"I will never...*ever*...do this again for you," she declared solemnly. "Don't even think about it."

The young dealer came back. I handed him the money and he passed the heroin to me through the window. I thanked him and we left.

True to her word, Mary never again rode along with me in the big Caddie, pretending to be associated with Sonny Sonetti.

The scariest situation I ever encountered as an undercover narc occurred in Detroit. And the threat wasn't from a dealer, but a unit in the Detroit Police Department infamously known as "the Big Four."

I was walking down the street with an informant to go make a buy. The guy was wearing a prison issue jacket. The Big Four wheeled up next to us in an unmarked car. The team was comprised of one uniformed officer who drove and three of the biggest, meanest looking guys you could imagine. The unit was known in the poor, black neighborhoods of Detroit for not caring a wit about constitutionally guaranteed rights. They were notorious for breaking down doors without warrants, for threatening wives and girlfriends, for beating suspects senseless—whatever it took to put the fear of God in people that vengeance was theirs.

Back then, Detroit ran one of the toughest, rough-and-tumble police departments in the country. The Big Four was one of two units in the city that was universally feared; the other was STRESS— which stood for "Stop the Robberies, Enjoy Safe Streets." STRESS units typically planted a decoy, a plainclothes cop sitting in a doorway of an abandoned building, dressed and slumped as if he was a worthless drunk. The bait was a twenty-dollar bill hanging out of his shirt pocket. The unit was primed for purely opportunistic crimes: somebody from the streets passing by, seeing the money, and, on impulse, lifting it. Whereupon team members on surveillance would immediately spring from hiding and demand the culprit to halt. As was often the case, the surprise prodded the person to run. The team members were notorious for drawing their weapons and firing, resulting in numerous deaths.

In August 1963, busloads of blacks from the Detroit inner city traveled to Washington to hear Dr. Martin Luther King Jr. deliver his "I Have a Dream" speech at the Lincoln Memorial. The speech inspired both faith and hope to "keep on keeping on" despite the obstacles. But when King was murdered the next spring, the suppressed anger and resentment among blacks exploded all across the country. Nowhere was this perhaps more dramatic then in Detroit. It was later speculated that the huge Detroit riots were fueled in part by the simmering rage over the long-term abuse perpetrated by these two police department teams.

For me, walking down a Detroit street with an easily recognized ex-con churned a primitive fear deep inside when the Big Four unit rolled up beside us.

"A fucking ex-con," one of them called out. "How long you been out, asshole?"

I was terrified. They had no reason to know who I was or what I did. It was bad enough my being with an ex-con. But I was also carrying a small, concealed .32-caliber pistol tucked into the front of my pants. The three muscle guys on the team separated us, banging us up against the car, with me on the driver side. I knew that if they found my gun, it was going to turn ugly fast.

The uniformed driver was still behind the wheel. I hoarsely whispered to him that I was a federal undercover narcotics agent. And that I had a gun tucked into my chinos. I told him I was working a deal.

For some reason, he believed my story. The driver told his partners I was clean. The Big Four maintained my cover. We were roughed up, but we didn't end up lying on the ground bleeding profusely. The encounter probably even gave me added cred on the streets. Overall, I considered myself extremely lucky. Things could have easily gone south. It was an encounter that remained vivid in my memory for years.

CHAPTER TEN

A "Kidnapping," Bongs, and Car Crashes

Being an undercover narc wasn't always so onerous. There were moments that were, in fact, quite the contrary.

One such moment occurred when I'd driven over to Canada to set up a buy. The deal didn't happen, so I turned around and headed back to Detroit, my surveillance team trailing in an unmarked car. Together we approached the international checkpoint at the Ambassador Bridge between Windsor, Ontario, and Detroit. I was directed to pull over and asked for my driver's license.

As I was siting there, a frightened, raspy voice from inside my car started pleading pitifully. "Help. I'm being kidnapped. I'm tied up in the trunk."

The US border agent immediately drew his weapon and stepped back. "Out of the car. *Now!*"

I did as I was told, hands raised. "I'm a Federal Bureau of Narcotics undercover agent." The border agent signaled for backup.

The two bureau surveillance agents in the other car behind me got out and jogged over, flashing their badges. They vouched for me, earnestly apologizing to the border guard. They explained how they'd used the hidden radio in my car to play the prank. The border agent absolutely failed to see the humor of it. We all were lectured strenuously. My two partners swore it would never happen again.

"Best not!" the border agent barked.

We were lucky to be let go with only a warning.

Another time I was working a deal to buy marijuana in Detroit. Before selling me anything, the dealer insisted I smoke a joint with him. I told him I wasn't in the mood, but he was unrelenting. My resistance made him suspicious. So I said okay.

The guy had a coconut shell, which had been hollowed out and taped together. There were small holes drilled in both ends. He put a fat joint in a hole at one end and lit it, then took a deep inhalation from a hole at the other end. He passed the coconut bong to me. I took it, pretending to marvel at the ingenuity of the thing. I couldn't help but notice, however, that the end you drew on was smudged with several shades of old lipstick. It was nasty looking, enough to turn your stomach. But I raised it, put it to my lips, and took a hit. It was very strong. I passed it back and he took a hit, then passed it back to me again. I took a toke and gave it back, saying that was enough for me. We did the deal and I left.

I went out and got in my Caddie. I was flying. High as a goose. I couldn't remember a summer day in Detroit more beautiful. I started the Caddie and eased it out into traffic. I cruised down the street, enjoying the rush of air through the open windows. Maybe three-quarters of a mile on, I stopped for a traffic light. A bureau surveillance detail pulled up next to me.

"McClaran, what are you doing?" the agent in the passenger seat called to me. I looked over, grinning.

"How you guys doin'?" I asked, looking out at them through glassy eyes.

"What the hell, McClaran? You're fried!"

My grin widened further. "Yeah, I know."

"Geeze. You were supposed to pull in back there at the shopping center."

"Sorry," I said, still grinning. "I'm friggin' stoned."

"No shit!" Both of them were cracking up. When they regained control, the one riding shotgun mustered a serious scowl.

"Pull over, dirtbag. You're under arrest." And the two of them started howling again.

When we later busted the guy, we took the coconut bong into evidence. After he was sentenced and put away, I managed to get a hold of it. I kept it for years, packing it from one place to another. I used to show it to friends when I told the story behind it. Finally, the nasty thing just sort of disintegrated and I had to throw it away.

Getting high was *not* part of the job. But getting into and out of trouble was. I was good at it—and lucky. You needed to be both to succeed and to survive.

One place I got into—but only once—was the home of a big dealer who went by the name of Manny. Manny lived in a relatively modest, quiet Detroit neighborhood. The one time I was there was to make a buy, which was very unusual for him to allow someone to come to the house to do a deal. I wasn't there long, but long enough to note the three steel bars that slotted into cradles either side of the front door. I was not surprised, as it was common for dealers to fortify their homes and wherever else they regularly transacted business, this to thwart a raid, buying them time to flush whatever they had down the toilet. Getting in when we were set to bust Manny was not going to be easy.

One of the other things I'd happened to notice, however, was that there was a bright streetlight in front of Manny's house. He had two cars: the "drug car" he used when he was out doing business, and his Sunday ride, a nice Cadillac. Manny always parked his drug car in the driveway, but his Sunday car he always parked out front, directly under the streetlight to ward off anybody tampering with it.

In a strategy session about how we were going to make the bust, I suggested that we fake a car accident in the middle of the night, where someone smashes into Manny's Sunday ride. It was agreed that this was likely the best strategy we had.

So we rolled up in Manny's neighborhood in the middle of the night. One of the local cops who were with us was a female officer. Everyone got in position in the shadows. Then she started banging two trashcan lids together like she was playing "The Star Spangled Banner," screaming, "*What have I done?! What have I done?!*" She made it sound like the world's worst car crash.

Manny's porch light snapped on. We could hear the steel bars barricading the door being thrown aside. Manny came tearing out the front door and down the walk in an undershirt and skivvies.

We had him in bright spotlights before he reached the curb. We commanded him to raise his hands. He stood bewildered for a moment before realizing what had happened. With his arms raised, he hazarded a backward glance toward the house, at the front door that yawned open as if in a welcoming gesture.

World's worst car crash? Not so much. But it was definitely a bad crash for Manny. He knew he was going away for a long time.

CHAPTER ELEVEN

Change Over

I was nearing eighteen months stationed in Detroit—the same length of duty as in Philadelphia—and I started to worry about getting transferred again. Agents had absolutely no say as to when or where they'd be reassigned. I'd sensed that the bureau was interested in placing me in New York City, one of the key entry points for heroin into the country. I wasn't bothered that New York would be a tough assignment, but I didn't want to move my family there. The Big Apple held zero appeal to me. So I started thinking about alternatives.

My girls were now seven and five. To date, I'd miss out on virtually all of their lives. I didn't know what they liked for breakfast, what they liked to wear, or who their friends were. In contrast, I knew from personal experience the painful hole an absent father can cause in a child's life. It wasn't that I was completely gone, never to be seen for years at a stretch, but I was *virtually* gone from their daily lives. Mary was an incredibly loving, attentive mother. She filled in for me in my absence without ever complaining—to me or about me to the girls. I think she admired and valued what I did. When the kids asked her what I did, saying their friends were curious, she said tell to them, "My daddy is out catching bad guys."

I had missed so much. I wanted to be a bigger part of their lives. I was also restless. I had always loved a challenge. And I was ambitious. So I started to consider leaving the Federal Bureau of Narcotics.

I happened to see an ad in *Police Chief* magazine for a chief's position in Harvey, Illinois. At the time, I wasn't even sure where Harvey was. I did a little research and decided on a whim to apply for the job. I considered being invited for an interview a long shot, as I had absolutely no supervisory experience. I knew nothing about managing a department budget.

Still, it would be a challenge.

I was amazed when I got notice from the selection committee that it wanted me to come to Harvey for an interview.

Harvey was a city of about 30,000 people on the south side of Chicago. It had a checkered history of crime. The city was roughly 70 percent black and had a forty-member police force.

When I walked into the local high school in June 1966 for an interview, I was surprised to find a small crowd waiting. The interview panel included the mayor, the entire city council, the superintendent of schools, the prosecuting attorney, a representative from the local ministerial association, the publisher of the local paper, and a police chief from another city. They asked a lot of questions.

The committee seemed quite enamored by the fact that I was a federal agent, though I had to keep correcting them that I was in the Federal Bureau of Narcotics, not the FBI. They also were taken by the fact that I had a college degree in police administration. The educational requirement for the position was a high school diploma.

I told them that if I was hired, I saw the first duty as chief as selling the officers under my command on the importance of their role to the community, and that they should be proud of that duty and responsibility. I knew that there had been complaints by the officers union with the outgoing chief over working conditions. I told them that bolstering morale was critical. Once morale was raised and the officers had bought into the vital importance of their work, we would work together to sell our vision to the community. I was one of thirteen applicants—and the youngest. I was only thirty years old.

What started out as a whim resulted in their offering me the job. The *Harvey Tribune*, the local paper, announced the appointment in an article where they reported that I "epitomized a new breed of police chief." It went on to say that I was "younger and has practical police experience which is backed up by a university degree in police administration," and that the selection committee had given me an "excellent" rating. I started August 1.

On my first day as chief, the *Tribune* ran an editorial headlined, "Welcome to our Fair City, William McClaran." The editorial read in part, "There would be no point in advising him of the areas of concern in which we believe local law enforcement can be improved. First, it would be presupposing that he needs advice. Second, we believe that by the time his first week is concluded, he will become aware of these by simple exposure."

Truer words were never spoken. And it didn't even take a week.

CHAPTER TWELVE

Gangs and Gunshots

I greatly enjoyed waking up those first few mornings and having breakfast with Mary and the girls. Such a simple thing. So ordinary and normal for so many people, but I relished it like I was on extended vacation.

Of course, I wasn't. I had a sizable task ahead of me. I immediately busied myself with getting to know the officers under my command and taking mental inventory of the policies and the current workings of the department. And then on Thursday night, I got a call at home from the police dispatcher.

An officer had stopped to break up a throng of rowdy teenagers gathered at the Dixie Square shopping mall on the west side of town. Several storeowners had called to complain. Rather than heed the officer's request, the group started throwing rocks and bottles at him, forcing him to retreat.

"You need to get out there!" the rattled dispatcher said. "It's getting ugly. They've started breaking windows and are looting."

Being new to the job, I was forced to ask the most fundamental question of the moment: "How do I get there?"

When I arrived, there were already officers awaiting my instructions. I noticed one officer's nametag—"Hess"—and directed him to go scout the back of the building. As soon as he stepped around the corner, he was shot. Other officers ran to pull him back to safety. He had an entrance wound in his chest, and an exit wound under his arm. The crowd of seventeen-to-twenty-year-old black youth that had been making off with appliances and anything else they could carry scattered at the sound of gunshots.

It wasn't clear from where the assailant had fired. An ambulance was dispatched to take Hess to the hospital. We swept the area to make sure no rioters were still present. Then we took inventory of the damage to the stores and of what had been stolen. We secured the area, and I posted officers to guard the building through the night.

Around 1 a.m., another call came in. This time a nearby Montgomery Ward department store had been broken into and a number of rifles and shotguns had been looted. Though only two or three vandals had been sighted, not the mass from earlier in the evening, this incident greatly escalated the threat of the night's lawlessness. I was aware that Harvey had a very violent history, and the community was deeply split by racial tensions. There were numerous rival black gangs, including the Harvey Rangers and the Dixmore Disciples. I suspected we were now potentially dealing with a very dangerous situation.

We began to receive reports of widespread vandalism. Several cars driving through town were rocked and had windshields shattered. Building and streets were spray-painted with gang tags, and someone dumped paint into the Harvey Park public pool. We patrolled all night, responding to disturbances and reports of further vandalism.

Things were quieter by dawn, but vandalism and looting sprang up again the next night and continued through the following night as well. I had nearly the full force out on patrol. The city was tense— or more precisely, the constant low-level tension that was ever present was massively elevated. The riot and resulting aftermath of vandalism and looting was not an isolated incident in the history of Harvey. As reported in one article about the riot, the disturbance mirrored a similar event only two years before, which the reporter referred to as the "1964 nightmare."

The article went on to state, "That outburst produced its stinging effect on commerce, on human relations, and on overall relations of those two fine communities" (Harvey and Dixmore). The current riot had "rekindled [the fear of] the hoodlum element."

The precipitating incident at the mall, we determined, was caused by a contingent of the Dixmore Disciples. The rivalry between the Rangers and the Disciples was extremely violent, with tit-for-tat antagonism. One infamous incident involved a group of Rangers that had loaded into an ice cream truck and driven over to Dixmore to cruise the Disciples' hangout—whereupon Rangers had opened fire from the rolling truck, shooting up the clubhouse.

Harvey's hiring of a "federal agent" as the new chief was part of the city's hope to bring greater order to the community. It was clear that I had a big job ahead of me. It was hard to shake the weight that my decisions as chief carried grave risks, including the danger of officers being shot. My dream of eating breakfast and dinner every day with my family lasted all of the first three days on the job.

Fortunately, Officer Hess's wound was not life threatening, and he recovered and eventually returned to duty. I was interviewed by the newspaper at the end of my first week on the job, and was quoted as ironically stating that the first week was "mildly trying."

The *Tribune*'s editorial for the week gave the department high marks. "Our police department handled the situation wonderfully and effectively well under our new, young professional administrator. He proved he was no novice at police command. The situation was quickly contained to a small area with damage and monetary loss held to a minimum. Unfortunately one of our law enforcement officers was forced to spill his blood before peace and order was restored."

Peace and order after a fashion. The city was still as racially divided as ever, and peace and order were very fragile in the aftermath. And I was far busier working to maintain control on things while also laboring to bring modern policing policies and practices to the department. Fortunately, my constant presence on the scene throughout the three-day disruption won me favor with those under my command. I was now viewed as one of them—that I was not a chief who remained separate and apart, but was willing to do myself everything that I asked of them.

CHAPTER THIRTEEN

"Harvey Heroes"

After we got the city quieted down, I spent the next several weeks speaking to various community groups. I wanted people to get to know me, as well as wanting to inform them of the changes I intended to bring to the department. I felt that this was a great opportunity to enact some of my earliest instincts as a police officer, going back to my time on the Grand Rapids force. I intended for the department to be more fully engaged with the community. In all my presentations before groups, I always greatly emphasized my view that police were first and foremost public servants.

I told people that there would be numerous changes, but that I planned to put them in place gradually. One of the first priorities was to completely update the department's policies and procedures, which hadn't been revisited since the Depression. We started a process where everyone in the department gave input and had their views heard. Together, we were defining how they were going to conduct themselves in doing their jobs. Most critically, I wanted to ensure that the department and the changes envisioned got buy-in from patrolmen from the start. I was guided in this by my belief that the men on the street knew a lot more about what they faced every day than I did.

High on the list would be training for all officers in all phases of police work; there was none being conducted currently. This would include internal training led by officers with various areas of expertise, and also granting leave so that officers could attend courses taught elsewhere. Internally, I set about implementing weekly sessions using the training program outlined by the International Association of Chiefs of Police (IACP), a standard used by over a thousand law enforcement agencies across the country. This program covered the gamut, from police standards to arrest and search procedures, to crime investigation, to handling of juveniles and nonconformists, and to dealing with dangerous drugs, mental illness, and other issues. A big piece of it was report writing. My goal was to streamline reporting while also making daily reporting mandatory. But we would implement the use of standard forms, and give instruction on the use of standard terminology.

I divided the city into four districts. We stepped up recruiting of new officers, and also started a review of the department pay scale. Additionally, we immediately put in effect a crackdown on juvenile curfew violations. All youth under eighteen were required to be off the streets from 10:30 p.m. to 6:00 a.m., unless accompanied by an adult. Curfews are fundamentally a means of controlling behavior. Before I was hired, enforcement was almost nonexistent.

We updated the fleet of patrol cars. And we requisitioned helmets, which were always to be worn. This greatly reduced the threat of injury from rock-throwing youths, for which there was an ongoing history of unprovoked incidents. All these programs and planned changes were set in motion by November—after only four months of my being on the job.

The plan for 1967 included continued training and the hiring of additional officers. Starting pay was increased from $500 to $540 a month. We also had plans to add a computerized system for identifying the location and status of every officer out on patrol. To augment coverage, we planned to add three additional squad cars so that we could have at least seven cars on the streets at any given time.

Officers on the Harvey force welcomed the changes and heartily embraced them. We spent a lot of time talking about public relations. I had always believed that the majority of people that you encounter in your work as a policeman are law abiding and decent.. As a consequence, it was imperative that we didn't stereotype people based on race or where they lived.

Not only were the officers receptive to the changes, but so too were the mayor and city council; both were extremely supportive of nearly everything I proposed. One of the first things we did was put a stop to the Dixmore police setting up speed traps in Harvey and ticketing drivers within our city limits.

Harvey had a history of violence. Shooting, stabbing, looting, and vandalism were prevalent. Before I arrived, there was one incident where two fourteen-year-old girls were beaten by a gang of boys while a crowd of a hundred watched. Soon after I came to Harvey, we had someone drive by the backside of the bleachers at Thornton Field, the high school football stadium, during a game and randomly fire a shotgun up into the stands. Nobody was killed, but several people were injured. Football games were often a flash point for trouble. One week that first fall, one of the Thornton High football players had his life threatened, with someone brandishing a gun in the school parking lot. We typically had a large contingent at the games, but that week we turned out in full force, blocking off streets, preventing any traffic to pass near the stadium.

I made it a point to see the city up close and personal, going out on patrol many nights with my officers, answering calls with them, responding to emergencies, and handling incidents on the swing shift. I was not a leader who sat in an office behind the safety and security of a big desk.

That January, a freak blizzard struck, totally shutting down the city. Late in the day, I got a call that a gang of youth was again smashing windows at the mall. Several stores were being looted, including furniture, grocery, and liquor stores. It was obvious that the vandals thought since the streets were blocked and impassable due to the heavy snowfall, there was little risk of police showing up to stop them.

I immediately called the public works department and asked what they had that could get through the snow. They sent a dump truck over, and my men and I climbed up into the bed and directed the driver to take us to the mall. I wasn't going to let the snowstorm stop us from doing our job. We rolled in and surprised the looters, making several arrests in quick order. That action dispelled any notion that the Harvey police were only fair-weather defenders of law and order.

My men worked around the clock over the next three days responding to calls from stranded and distressed citizens. I instructed my men that we were to serve people doing anything they needed. We received thousands of calls over a seventy-two-hour period. We used all available vehicles at our disposal, including anything with four-wheel drive, mail trucks fitted with chains, and tow trucks. We took people without heat to warm shelters, brought food and medicine to people who were shut in, and provided a sense of hope to the entire community that we all would get through the storm together.

For our efforts, officers in the department were publicly deemed the "Harvey Heroes." The *Tribune* ran stories about our exploits for days after the city finally was able to dig out from the storm. It was a golden moment in the history of the department. Everyone on the force was proud to be a Harvey patrolman. And there were countless citizens who truly looked upon us as heroes for the heroic lengths we went to serve them.

The department was on its ways to being perceived in a new light, as an invaluable asset to the life of the community.

CHAPTER FOURTEEN

Into the Fire—Benton Harbor

I got a call shortly before Christmas 1967 from a former professor of mine in the criminal justice program at Michigan State. He told me that the mayor of Benton Harbor in western Michigan was looking to hire a new police chief. The mayor had asked if he knew anybody who might be interested, and my friend had given him my name. I was told to expect a call.

I had been in Harvey about a year and a half, and I had accomplished most of what I had set out to do in terms of department reorganization and instituting ongoing officer training. The possibility of moving back to Michigan appealed to both my wife and me. When the mayor called, I told him I was indeed interested in considering the position, but that I needed more particulars about the job and the community. He sent these, and we subsequently arranged to meet.

Benton Harbor had a larger police department than Harvey. It was about 150 miles west of Detroit on Lake Michigan. I knew that it once had been a favorite getaway for Al Capone, who had even thrown himself a going-away party at the Vincent Hotel that still stood on Main Street before he went off to spend his last days at the federal pen.

Mary and I drove the eighty miles around the bottom of the lake so that I could meet with the city manager. I'll never forget driving down the main street that first afternoon and encountering a man standing in the middle of the street with a long knife in his hand.

"This looks *very* interesting," I said enthusiastically to my wife.

"What? A guy with a knife in the middle of the street?"

"The whole thing," I said.

"You're crazy."

"Yeah, I know," I said, smiling excitedly. My first impression was that this was going to be a challenge. And I loved challenges.

I met with the Mayor Wilbur Smith and City Manager Don Stewart. They were very forthcoming about the problems the city faced. There was a lot of racial tension and a lot of crime. The city had about 16,500 citizens, a decrease of about 2,000 over the previous two decades. Roughly 90 percent of the population was black. Just across the Saint Joseph River was the city of Saint Joseph, a very white and affluent community. The mayor and city manager told me that the Benton Harbor Police Department was desperately in need of updating—from top to bottom.

"We need to modernize operations. Develop a training program for the patrolmen," Stewart said.

I told him I'd just done that in Harvey. And that I wanted the job. I started as chief of police in February 1968.

I was barely on the job two months when Martin Luther King Jr. was assassinated in Memphis, Tennessee, on April 4. At the moment the news reached me, I was conducting the department's regular Thursday evening riot training workshop. I told the officers what had happened and to stand by. I went downtown and encountered a large group that was gathering. I tried to talk with them, to encourage them to stay calm and not do anything rash. The crowd swept right past me.

In less than an hour, a large contingent of the black community had amassed and had started marching through downtown. The crowd became unmanageable. Molotov cocktails were being tossed indiscriminately, starting numerous fires. They firebombed one of the police cruisers. I immediately ordered that all city gas stations be closed. We were fast struggling to keep things from getting completely out of hand and—quite literally—exploding.

The city of Saint Joseph immediately ordered that the drawbridge over the river that separated the two municipalities be raised to prevent the mayhem from spreading there. The police department from nearby Benton Township came to our assistance. The state police came in as well.

We managed to get through the night. By early the next morning, things had quieted considerably. But the streets were virtually empty, as few businesses chose to open that day. Come dark, however, marauding bands started vandalizing again. As a department, we changed shift scheduling, keeping only a skeleton crew on days, with most of the force out on patrol at night. Though things in Benton Harbor were bad, it was much worse elsewhere around the country. This included fierce rioting in Detroit, where long-simmering rage among blacks there over the treatment they received by the Detroit police department led to large swathes of the city being torched every night. The situation was tense in Benton Harbor, but things eventually began to settle down after several days.

A couple of weeks after the riot, I asked if I could speak at the Sunday service in one of the prominent black churches in town. Some welcomed me, but there was still a lot of tension just below the surface.

Standing before the Sunday congregation, I said I knew some people felt I shouldn't be there. "And there are some who say you shouldn't have invited me." But I told them it was vitally important that we keep our "doors" open to one another, and that we listen to what each other has to say.

"Halleluiah!" rang out a lone voice. I drew courage from it. I continued to speak to the need that we listen to complaints from all parties, and that we strive to move forward together.

"Halleluiah!" came the refrain again, this time from several voices. I could feel the tension in the church begin to ease.

I spoke about the need for us to learn to trust one another, because at heart, we all wanted the same thing: a safe community in which to live, and to raise and educate our kids.

Halleluiahs rose up throughout the church.

I told them that I appreciated their invitation to hear me speak. And that I intended to speak at my own church the following Sunday. And also that I was going to tell them the same thing. "Amen," "That's right," and "You tell 'em" rolled forth from the gathering.

While I knew that I hadn't solved all the problems by standing up in one church on one Sunday, as everyone began to file out after the service ended, I felt that a very different mood had taken hold in that congregation. Several people came up and shook my hand and thanked me for coming. I thanked them for having me. And I promised that it wouldn't be the last time that they heard from their chief of police. I told them that we were all in this together.

CHAPTER FIFTEEN

George Wallace "Comes" to Town...and More Riots

We barely got through the riots when another seismic wave seized the city. I suppose I should have expected it, but it caught me completely by surprise.

George Wallace, the firebrand, former governor of Alabama, and staunch segregationist, was running for president that year. And his staff had come to Benton Harbor and opened a campaign office downtown. It was like an echo of the shot that killed King in Memphis the month before. The reverberations rippled through the black community with frightening speed.

A group of blacks came in to see me. They said that George Wallace ought not to be allowed to have an office in Benton Harbor. They demanded that he be made to leave. I told them that Wallace had a constitutional right to be here, just like anybody else. They told me that they were going to picket his presence. I told them that they, too, had a constitutional right to do that, but that they couldn't block the sidewalk or the entrance to his campaign office.

I was in the office late the following day when my secretary rushed in to tell me that there was a large, angry crowd of about two hundred people out in the parking lot.

"They're demanding to know why you won't let them picket."

I got up, came around my desk, and started to go out to address them.

"You can't go out there, Chief," she pleaded. "They'll kill you."

"Nobody's going to kill me," I assured her as I continued toward the door.

"But, Chief, it's too dangerous."

The crowd was definitely in an ugly mood. I found my way through them to a low rise at the back of the parking lot. I walked to the top and turned around to face them.

"You lied to us. You said you weren't going to arrest anybody if we picketed Wallace's office," someone yelled. The crowd grew rancorous.

I raised my hands for quiet. "I didn't lie to you," I said loudly. "Nobody's going to get arrested for peacefully picketing in front of the Wallace campaign office."

"That's not what we hear," shouted another. "Yeah," rang a chorus of other voices. Everybody was talking over everybody else.

I raised my hands again for quiet. "I did not lie to you. And I will *never* lie to you. You may not always like what I have to say, but you'll never hear me lie. *That*, I promise."

"That's what you say, but we heard your police are planning to arrest us," one person in the back of the crowd yelled out.

I shook my head. "If you're peaceful—and obey the law, you've got every right to picket. And nobody in my police department is going to arrest you. Like I said—I promise you."

The group began to quiet down. People were turning to murmur to one another, taking it in, talking about what to do next. I stood watching them. Some on the edges began to curl away to leave. Then more. Within five minutes, the whole crowd had turned and was heading home again.

I shook my head in amazement. Nobody said this job was going to be easy. Least of all me. The challenge of it was what had originally attracted me. As for having friendly breakfasts with my wife and two girls and dinners hearing about their days—it didn't look like that was going to happen anytime soon.

The surface tension following the assassination of Martin Luther King Jr. abated significantly, as did the emotions stirred by the Wallace campaign opening an office in downtown Benton Harbor. Robert Kennedy being assassinated in early June, on the night he won the California Democratic primary for president, was a shock, but it didn't generate the seismic repercussions that the earlier two events had sparked. At the start of summer, I felt fairly well versed as to what might lie ahead. I began to have confidence that we'd weathered the worst. I turned my attention to focusing on the much-needed reorganization of the Benton Harbor police department.

And then July came along and smacked us square in the face.

This time the trouble was ignited by a couple of black teenagers who'd been attending a dance at the local youth center. In the middle of the dance, they left and went to a nearby bar wanting to buy alcohol. When the proprietor of Babe's Lounge refused to serve them, a brief fight broke out, and the two were escorted out of the bar. They went back to the dance and enlisted their friends to join them in settling the score. As soon as the contingent entered the lounge, the owner insisted that they all take it outside. Once outside, the gang of youths began to beat the bar owner. Police were called and the gang of kids and a crowd of onlookers scattered. Not long after, gunshots were heard in a nearby neighborhood.

The tension that had been simmering for months exploded yet again. Rampaging youth began stoning cars and breaking storefront windows. Fires were set. What had started out as an isolated incident quickly flared out of control across the city.

I called in support from five different area law enforcement agencies, including the police from Benton Township and Saint Joseph, the Berrien County Sherriff's Department, and the state police. From my experience in Grand Rapids, I knew that local police and the state police in Michigan had always enjoyed a strong working relationship. This was certainly true that night in Benton Harbor, as well. But the police chief from Saint Joseph began remarking how he and his men intended to simply "take out" the troublemakers. This was not a response that would be conducive to quelling the disturbance, and I ordered them back across the bridge to their own jurisdiction.

The violence raged for three days. There were numerous fire bombings, especially of the residences of prominent authority figures. This included the home of Municipal Judge Elizabeth Forhan—for the second time that year—and Justice of the Peace Les Price's home. Mayor Wilbur Smith's house was also firebombed. In addition, a fire was set at the junior high school. Firefighters were called to respond to over half a dozen fires that night.

Much of the city's commercial district was shuttered during the three-day rampage. At one point, my patrolmen and a contingent from the state police marched down Main Street in full force and began arresting everyone they encountered. Over seventy arrests were made during the disturbance, including thirty arrests made the third night, most all of them teenagers. Rioting crowds grew as large as five hundred people. They were met by over two hundred police from several jurisdictions, and one hundred fourteen state troopers. Gradually, we gained the upper hand. Finally, by the fourth day, the city was largely brought back under control, with the exception of a few minor disturbances. Things were relatively quiet, but the peace never felt very deep.

My first six months on the job as chief of police in Benton Harbor were anything but routine. And I was out of the house all hours of the day and night. The job was clearly all consuming; as a consequence, my family saw little of me.

CHAPTER SIXTEEN

Police Riots and First Amendment Rights

There were a lot of internal police department issues that demanded my attention, from personnel and staffing, to department organizational structure. Given all the racial upheaval in the city in recent weeks, I was shocked one afternoon overhearing a black detective interrogating a suspect in an office across from mine.

"Listen, nigger," the detective said. I knew the detective to do good work, to be 100 percent committed to being a part of the team, but to me, his language was way out of line. After the suspect was released, I walked over to his office and asked him how things were going. He said things were going pretty well.

"I couldn't help but overhear you talking to that suspect," I said.

He nodded.

"And though I have no problem with your work, I can't have you using that kind of language. It's totally unacceptable."

"But he *is* a nigger," the detective said defensively. "He's a troublemaker. I've had run-ins with him for a long time."

"You're entitled to your opinion," I said. "But you can't use that language while you're on the job. There's no debate about it. Are we clear?"

He nodded. "Understood. You won't hear it again from me."

———

As I'd done in Harvey, I organized the city into four districts, each shift headed by a commander who reported to me. We also updated the policy and procedures manual, and we started an ongoing training program for all officers. I constantly stressed to my men that we were public servants, and as such, we were here to do more than simply lock up the bad guys. The department created a youth bureau, which I had long thought was always money well spent. I set in motion plans to double the number of patrol cars on the streets during the afternoon and evening hours, and I assigned more patrolmen to the night shift.

We got a $25,000 grant to remodel headquarters and began major updates to simplify access and flow in the building. The building originally had four different entrances, and it was common to find people from off the streets wandering through the halls, trying to find where they needed to go. We eliminated three of the entrances and improved the main entrance so that it was clearly obvious this was the one entrance the public could use. We also created new offices for the detective bureau and new interrogation rooms, and we centralized all records in one new area. As it happened, we ran out of money before all the work was done. So everyone in the department voluntarily stepped up to finish painting the interior—all on our own time. It was clear testament of the officers' commitment to the changes I was making.

The 1968 Democratic Presidential Convention was held in Chicago. The anti–Vietnam War movement was in full force, feeling newly empowered because President Lyndon Johnson had decided not to seek reelection. There was a great mood of distemper in the country, fueled in part by the war and by the assassinations of Martin Luther King Jr. and presidential hopeful Robert Kennedy. There had been over a hundred riots that summer across the country. Senator Eugene McCarthy of Minnesota was the standard-bearer for the anti-war movement, but it wasn't likely that he would win the nomination over Vice President Hubert Humphrey.

Chicago Mayor Richard Daley had had hopes to use the convention to showcase his city. But protesters arrived en masse in Chicago the first week in August. And the Chicago Police Department was ready for them. Violent clashes between protestors and police were featured as headline stories in the nightly news, with vivid—and shocking—film footage showing club-wielding cops overpowering and beating young people to the ground in the streets of Chicago. Humphrey ended up winning the nomination, but there was little jubilation. The four-day violence became widely known as "the Chicago police riot"—maybe not the first of such in US history, but perhaps the most memorable, given the nightly television news coverage that streamed into millions of American homes.

I was interviewed by the local Benton Harbor paper about the convention, and I think I shocked many with my comments. I was quoted as saying, "I was a little sickened by what I saw on television. The provocation was immense, but the role of police should not be punitive. [Their job] is protection of life and property, with arrests when necessary, and use of force only when required. You have to use force according to the law. You can't rise above the law. We all want constitutional guarantees."

It set me a part from many police chiefs across the nation, as well as from many of the citizens of Benton Harbor. But order without the rule of law was worse than hollow. It gravely undermined the foundation of civil society.

CHAPTER SEVENTEEN

Liberal-Minded Cop

My two daughters, Pat and Lynn, were nine and seven when we moved to Benton Harbor. We lived on a quiet street with great neighbors, and both girls walked to school. The city being predominantly black made them a part of the clear minority at school. Lynn was the only white student in her classroom, and Pat and another girl were the only whites in theirs. Though both my daughters were aware of racial tensions, they weren't particularly troubled by their own uniqueness. Tolerance was an issue that both my wife and I valued and talked about, and the girls likewise embraced it. That's not to say that there weren't incidents at school that reflected the tensions and violence in the city at large. On occasion, my girls had legitimate reason to feel unsafe.

There was much greater tension and violence in the upper grades, with a student being shot and killed at the high school. As the shooter was leaving the building, he blew out a trophy case on his way down the hall. There was never any question who did it, and we arrested the kid at home later that day. The school was closed for two weeks. Numerous community meetings were held to discuss what to do to stem such violence. For several weeks following the school's reopening, we had officers patrolling the halls. We maintained the security detail until students began to once again feel that it was safe to be there.

We always had twenty to thirty patrolmen at the football games to temper antagonism between opposing schools. For some reason, the bands were common targets of rock throwers, especially the tuba players, with gang factions perpetually picking them out to target, trying to lob rocks into the large round bells above their heads.

I was at my desk one day when my secretary came in to say that there was a taxi driver who wanted to talk to me. I told her to show him in.

He said I might be interested to know that he'd just dropped off a fare that included two men. And the whole time they were in the taxi, they were talking about killing me. I didn't know quite what to make of it, how serious it might be, but it was disconcerting. Enough so that I called the city attorney, Sam Henderson, who was a neighbor and a personal friend, to ask what he thought I should do.

"Do you have a will?" he deadpanned.

That evening when I drove home, having to pass by his house, I saw that he'd posted a sign in his yard: "The chief lives two doors down," with an arrow pointing toward my house. Sam definitely had a unique sense of humor.

Every Christmas holiday in Benton Harbor, the Hendersons; another family, the Sondees; and Mary, the girls, and I would book a short stay in the local Holiday Inn. It had an indoor heated pool. Both families had kids about our girls' ages. The kids stayed in their own rooms, and the grown-ups likewise had rooms of our own. There at the inn we would all just hang out for a couple of days. The girls loved it. They loved having a heated pool, their own room, and ordering room service. It made them feel grown up. In addition to Thanksgiving and Christmas Day, it was always one of the annual high points for our family.

Bringing greater law and order to Benton Harbor was indeed a challenging task. The city routinely had over six hundred stabbings and shootings every year. But serious crime came down 11 percent the first year I was there, while nationwide, it went up. We broke up gambling operations that had existed with impunity for years. And in 1971, crime came down another 7 percent.

The Benton Harbor Kiwanis Club named me Citizen of the Year in 1969. The Bar Association of Berrien County awarded me with its Liberty Bell Award for "community service through strengthening freedom under the law."

In 1972, the local paper wrote an editorial about what it saw as my unique style: "McClaran is regarded as a liberal-minded cop. He's perhaps among a minority of officers that believe that Supreme Court decisions (Miranda) protecting individual rights have not been detrimental to police work." Then it quoted me from an interview: "'You, too, would want those rights if you were arrested,' he told a group of Twin City business men."

By the spring of 1972, I had met much of the challenge and had accomplished what I'd set out to do in coming to Benton Harbor. Again, I saw an ad in *Police Chief* magazine for a position in Portland, Maine. As a kid I'd spent time in Maine during the summer at a "camp" belonging to relatives who lived in Cambridge, Massachusetts. I applied for the job.

Dr. Martin Lew, superintendent of Benton Harbor schools, wrote me a letter of recommendation. In part, his letter read, "I have participated in some hot public meetings with Bill McClaran. He never loses his temper. He gives straight, logical answers that don't always satisfy the critics, but they [the critics] rarely question his integrity."

I flew to Portland for an interview. The afternoon before the interview, I called a cab to drive me around the city. What I saw amazed and intrigued me. One of the first things that caught my eye was a rack of clothes out on the sidewalk in front of a store. A simple enough thing, perhaps, but I'd never seen this in any of my earlier jobs. No one elsewhere would have been foolish enough to put merchandise unattended out on the sidewalk.

The other thing that caught my eye was a Portland policeman walking a beat. He was sauntering along enjoying the day. This wasn't what attracted me; what did was that he had a banana "holstered" in the pocket where his sap, or blackjack, was supposed to be. I smiled. Portland seemed like a very interesting change from Harvey and Benton Harbor. But it was obvious, too, that uniform standards—and who knew what else—needed some attention. I went back to my hotel thinking that if I was offered the position of chief, I would take it.

Perhaps Portland would finally offer me the opportunity for an interesting career posting that was also quiet and routine enough where I could spend more time with my family.

My father Lieutenant Commander William B. McClaran Sr., USNR. Photo taken prior to his taking command of the USS *Wiseman* DE-667 in 1944.

My mother Lois McClaran, my sister Joan, and me.
Family photo sent to my father in 1944.

Steele Corner School, outside of Rockford, Michigan. There was one teacher for six grades. I'm in the second row down, second from the right with whistle around my neck distinguishing me as the school safety captain, 1946.

Getting ready to walk my beat as an officer of the Grand Rapids, Michigan, Police Department. Late fall 1957.

"Mug" shot of Sonny Sonnetti in 1964. Used by Philadelphia Police detectives to show around bars where known heroin traffickers hung out, establishing my "street cred" as a badass.

PASSENGER		JAMES M. HARE Secretary of State	
1966 License No. AK-2341	Code	Wayne COUNTY OF OWNER	
William E. Sonetti NAME OF OWNER		UNINSURED FUND	
1400 E. Jefferson STREET ADDRESS		LICENSE FEE	
Detroit CITY	Michigan STATE	TITLE & TR. FEE	
1962 Cadillac YEAR MAKE	Convt. BODY STYLE	TAX	
62F110253 VEHICLE NO.	4480 WEIGHT	TOTAL	
William E. Sonetti OWNER SIGN HERE			
MICHIGAN PASSENGER REGISTRATION EXPIRES FEB. 28, 1967 MUST BE CARRIED IN VEHICLE OR BY DRIVER			3

Copy of the registration for Sonny's '62 Cadillac convertible, my "pimp car" in Detroit, 1966.

My daughters Pat and Lynn at home in Philadelphia, 1963.

Sonny getting ready to hit the streets in Detroit, 1965.

Official photo as Chief of Police in Harvey, Illinois, 1966.

Official photo as Chief of Police in Benton Harbor, Michigan, 1968.

Being honored as Kiwanis Club Citizen of the Year in 1969. Standing with the president of Kiwanis and another award recipient.

As Chief of Benton Harbor, talking to Detective Sergeant Al Edwards and Detective Elmer Rhodes.

Official photo as Chief of Police in Portland, Maine, 1972.

Being presented with the Crime Fighter of the Year
Award, 1976, by Batman and Robin.

My wife Mary and me with our son Will before his senior prom at Pine Tree Academy in Freeport, Maine, 2004.

Mary and me on Skellig Michael Island, Ireland, with Little Skellig behind us in 2005.

With my grown children, Lynn, Will, and Pat, celebrating my 70th birthday in Portland, Maine, 2004.

Musical group Alana, comprised of the O'Connor brothers: Anthony, Patrick, Sean, and Brendan, left to right respectively. Performing at O'Donoughues Pub in the Killarney Towers Hotel, Killarney, County Kerry, Ireland in 2006.

Patrick Anderson, Pat's son – my grandson, who is a gifted musician.

Family photo taken on the Dingle Peninsula, County Kerry,
Ireland, 2011. Left to right: Michael and Pat Ybarra; Lynn
Moriarty and her son and daughter, Michael and Erin Moriarty;
Will McClaran, Kevin Moriarty (Lynn's husband), and me.

A group of my students at the Southern Maine Technical College (now Southern Maine Community College) posing with me in my office, 2004.

Four former students, all in law enforcement in Maine, with me in Ireland, 2005. Left to right: Paul Gaspar, executive director, Maine Association of Police; Michael Sawyer, K-9 officer, Scarborough Police Department; Sgt. Paul Fenton, Cape Elizabeth Police Department; Lt. Robert Doherty, Portland Police Department; and me

Daughters Pat and Lynn, and me at Torc Waterfall
outside Killarney, County Kerry, Ireland in 2011.

Carole Ann Dunphe, my wife's closest friend, with her two daughters, Bernie
on the left, and Jackie. They're standing outside of an ancient "beehive
hut" dwelling on the Dingle Peninsula, County Kerry, Ireland, 2006.

My wife Mary's favorite beach in Ireland – Coomenoule Beach, Dingle Peninsula, Country Kerry. Our son Will and I scattered Mary's ashes there in June 2009, five months after her passing.

CHAPTER EIGHTEEN

Bringing Community Policing to Portland

I met with Portland City Manager John Menario. He was a very decent guy and I liked him immediately. He told me that what Portland was looking for in a chief was someone to bring its department fully into the twentieth century, with new policies and modern policing practices. The city was growing, with a current population of 66,000 citizens. The greater metro area had a population of about 190,000. There were 167 officers to cover twenty-two square miles in the department's jurisdiction, including three islands out in Casco Bay. Menario pointed out that the city was just about to break ground on a new headquarters building that would provide a foundation for a lot of opportunity to do things differently. The current headquarters on Federal Street dated back to the turn of the century.

I was thirty-six years old, one of 118 applicants for the job. And I was delighted when the city offered the position to me. My daughters were thirteen and ten, and though they both would miss their friends, they thought moving to Maine was an adventure. Pat, my oldest, was very excited to be moving to New England—she thought it sounded very exotic, moving to a place that had "England" in its name. Lynn was excited that it was near the ocean. We moved in July 1972, and I became the youngest chief in the city's history.

On my first day on the job, July 24, Menario and I turned the first shovels for the construction of the new headquarters building, budgeted at $2.3 million. I saw this as a symbolic act of being able to lay the foundation for a whole new way of policing, one that would build on my growing commitment to "community policing"—where the department was integral to the life of city, well beyond putting offenders in jail.

The first night on the job, I was out cruising the city, getting a better sense of what it was like at night. By in large, it was quiet. I was down into the Bayside area, between the new interstate freeway being built and the main business district, when a call from the dispatcher came through requesting an officer to a construction site on Marginal Way to investigate a report of possible prowlers. Since I was on Marginal Way, I headed toward the address. Next to the site was a large event tent. I got out just as an officer on duty pulled in and got out of his patrol car..

"You security?" he asked.

"Ah, kind of," I replied. He directed me to circle the building, which I did. Back out in front, I went into a large canvas event tent that was erected on the site. The patrolman was drinking some soda that had been left over.

"Is it clear?" he asked.

"Yeah." I watched him fill his cup again.

"Want anything? Help yourself."

I made a quizzical face. "Are you sure you're supposed to be doing that?"

He seemed to truly look at me for the first time.

"*Ah, god!*" he moaned. "You're the new chief, aren't you?" he said, setting the cup of soda down on the table.

A small smile lit my face. I nodded. "Yeah, I am."

The patrolman straightened to stand more formally before me.

"Why don't you finish checking things out and report back to the dispatcher," I said.

"Yes, sir."

Over the next several days, I saw the patrolman around the old headquarters building. He was always a little nervous in seeing me. I always smiled and nodded. I never called him into my office, never wrote him up. By my behavior, I let him know that the incident was just between the two of us. I knew that word would get around that the new chief was "okay." The department was already beginning to see that I expected a lot from them. But that I was also someone who was in this together with them, doing what was needed to serve the city.

I spent the first few weeks reading police reports to get a sense of things in the city. I happened to be in the jail area when two patrolmen brought in a black man. After he was booked and put in a cell, I asked the desk sergeant why the guy was arrested.

"The two officers pulled up at a traffic light, and while they were waiting for the light to change, they heard him say 'motherfucker' to someone he was talking to."

"Seriously?" I asked.

The sergeant looked at me, a bit puzzled. "Yeah," he responded simply. "We don't use that kind of language here."

"Where I come from, that's a greeting—'Hey, *mothafucker*!' That's not something we should be arresting people for."

The sergeant was surprised, but nodded in agreement. When the case came to court, the judge threw it out.

One of the first changes I instituted dealt with the handling of evidence. There was no secure, central area for holding criminal evidence. All the detectives kept evidence from the cases they were working in their desks. This was a simple fix: I designated one office as the evidence room, and everybody had to file what they had there. It was a small change, but it was indicative of the kinds of policies and practices that needed to be put in place.

Though I was busy, there wasn't the same kind of tension in the job—or in Portland—as there had been in my work in Harvey and Benton Harbor. I outlined my plans for the changes I intended to make in an interview with the *Portland Press Herald*.

"My first job will be to review the department as a whole in all its various phases, with an eye to seeing how good a product we're putting out and assessing how it can be better," I was quoted as saying. "I want my people to be in the *know*—especially as to the *why*—I was making the changes.

"I want the public to view me and the members of the police department as public employees, not a security society."

I went on to say that the last six years had been among the toughest in the country's history, in terms of the responsibilities of the police departments everywhere. "It's been a turbulent time, a time of social change."

I said that departments had been pressed to keep abreast of the things as they must, "but change is a difficult thing for many people to accept." I said much of the pressure for change had come from young people. "The young have questioned the so-called establishment, which the police are a part of. Some of the questions [they've put forward] have been embarrassing because we haven't had good answers. I think we can find the answers—and I think we should."

In another interview in another paper, I further articulated my approach to community policing: "Crime is a community problem, not a police problem. Enforcing the law is the policeman's job, but the causes and solutions to crime should involve the entire community."

In truth, Portland wasn't a high-crime city. It was just stuck in time in terms of its policies and its police organization. The first thing I did was look at the organization and how the department did things. One of the first changes I made was to create a bureau of crime prevention and community relations. Through speaking engagements around the city, I made people aware that we should all be involved in crime prevention. I stressed that the police department should not be apart *from* the community—but a part *of* it.

Under the previous chief, the city had hired an outside consultant to make recommendations regarding changes that should be made to the department. The consultant, a university professor, aided by a graduate student, had reviewed the organization and then developed a report that specified what they thought ought to be done. The report was passed on to me upon my becoming chief. I didn't see much value in any of the recommendations, but I happened to get to know the graduate student, Greg Hanscom, and liked him a lot. He had a keen mind and extremely strong people skills, as well as a strong instinct for community service and citizen participation. I hired him as my first administrative assistant.

One of the first big sets of changes I put in place—to ensure we provided better service and were truly a part of the community—was to reorganize the structure of the department. This gave us three new operating bureaus: field service, staff service, and crime prevention and community relations. The first two were commanded by deputy chiefs. The third was headed by a civilian director who had full authority and control over the officers in his bureau. I named

Frank Amoroso to head that bureau. I'd met Amoroso soon after coming to Portland. He had been working in another department in city government, and he impressed me. Under his command were the youth aid division, the police athletic league, and the community relations division, made up of the school liaison unit and the crime prevention unit.

One of the first things the community relations and crime prevention division did was conduct a series of door-to-door neighborhood surveys. We selected areas where there was both a high incidence of crime and of complaints against the department. Following the surveys, we held neighborhood meetings, inviting the citizens we'd spoken with to attend. The heads of all my bureaus and I sat before the groups to hear more about what they had to say, to respond to their questions, and to listen to their complaints. We saw the benefit of this as twofold: gathering more information, and building stronger bridges into the community.

One of the most significant things that came out of these efforts was our realization of the extent of dissatisfaction that existed over how complaints against the department were handled. Neighborhood residents knew firsthand that there was a pattern of disparity, something that the whole city had also recently become aware of through public revelations before I arrived. The revelations had created a minor scandal in the city. The attendees complained that if you were poor or lived in less affluent neighborhoods, complaints were not given the same importance as those that came from citizens living in the more upscale parts of town.

We promised change. One of the major things we did was put in place a formal, transparent procedure for handling complaints. And I stressed to the entire department the importance that people were not to be treated differently, nor their complaints given less attention, based on their socioeconomic status or where they lived.

Several initiatives were undertaken in the divisions under Amoroso's command. This included the creation of two teen centers in neighborhoods where there were high incidences of complaints against juveniles. The rules and policies at the centers were developed and supported by the kids themselves. We also started providing direct interaction with kids who might be having problems in school, causing disturbances, or being absent, with our involvement aimed at doing what was necessary to support them so that they'd attend, be attentive, and become successful students rather than troublemakers.

And we inaugurated a police athletic league, with officers assigned to oversee it. When the new police headquarters building eventually opened, we used the new gymnasium for many of the activities for the athletic league, including volleyball and basketball. In the summer, we also offered softball and organized trips to various state parks and beaches in the surrounding area.

Not everyone was taken with our emphasis on working to form closer ties to the community, especially with the youth of the city. Much of our activity with youth was focused on the kids from Munjoy Hill, an east-end neighborhood that was, at that time, predominantly composed of working-class and lower-income families. At one city council meeting, one counselor remarked that we spent too much time "playing with kids from the Hill, when you should be taking them to jail."

The changes I and my department were instituting clearly marked a new approach to policing, moving away from focusing solely on catching the bad guys and putting greater emphasis on community relations and community service. Our emphasis on the youth of the city was aimed at helping them be more integral to the life of their neighborhoods and the city; to provide them an opportunity to rub elbows and personally get to know police officers, coming to see them as people rather than uniformed strangers to be avoided on the streets; and to help them experience—and envision—a different way of life and of living in the community.

CHAPTER NINETEEN

Asserting Authority and Women Officers

Some months after assuming duties as chief of the Portland Police Department, there was a murder in the city. I naturally assigned a team from our department to handle the investigation. I was soon surprised, however, to learn that murders in our city were not within our jurisdiction to investigate. The task belonged to detectives from the Maine state police. This was made abundantly clear when the state detectives showed up and took over.

This greatly disturbed me, as I'd never heard of such a thing. I stood by to observe the state unit's handling of the case. Essentially what they singularly focused on was interviewing all of our officers who had any knowledge of the death. And then the "staties" gathered up all the evidence that we'd collected—and left.

I asked a deputy chief why the state got involved in a city matter. He said that was the way it had always been done. I made some inquiries that led me to contact the state attorney general. I asked him why this was the protocol. He said it was state policy. I asked him what I needed to do to have the policy changed. He told me that if I had a couple of my people trained and certified, he'd consider it.

So I sent two people for official homicide investigation training. After they were certified, the attorney general changed the policy whereby we would have jurisdiction to investigate murders in Portland. We formalized the handling of evidence and established a basic crime lab. Some while later, Bangor became the second city in Maine to become certified in a similar manner. The Maine state police, however, continued to handle all other murder investigations around the state.

I also initiated the psychological testing of candidates applying to become officers. The goal was to weed out applicants whose profiles revealed that they weren't ideal candidates, either in not being mature enough, or discovering that were situations where there were questions about their psychological fitness to become sworn officers of the law. The initial focus of the new psychological testing was on new recruits, but we eventually extended it to active officers as well. It was part of a larger program designed to provide me another critical resource in working with the force. If an officer had anger management issues, I could refer him to Dr. Norm Lyford, a local psychologist we put on retainer. He was also available for officers who were dealing with the emotional stress of the job or with stress at home. There was considerable resistance, however, from the members of the department to use Dr. Lyford's services. The prevailing, general culture of policing in this country had long stigmatized such practices. Such behavior was deemed "weak." I strongly felt that it was the right thing to do, so I continued to make Dr. Lyford available to the department.

Eventually, I also started a peer review process to support officers who were involved in violent engagements with citizens or perpetrators, especially where they had responded to horrific crime scenes or had been put in a situation where they had to use potentially lethal force.

This had deep roots going back to my first days as a patrolman in Grand Rapids, Michigan. Perhaps the most powerful personal experience for me was that time that my partner and I found a young suicide victim in the basement of his mother's home—and he turned out to be someone I knew fairly well. I instinctively stifled my emotional distress so that my partner wouldn't catch me crying.

Despite the personal satisfaction of being a good and decent cop, it is a pretty thankless job much of the time. A code of iron fortitude and the ability to deal with anything leads to the risk of building up a protective shield to keep emotional distress in check. Officers make sick jokes about the terrible things they witness, but they won't talk about their feelings. In fact, you strive to not have any feelings. Which is humanly impossible. And so officers are left with carrying the corrosive weight of such incidents sealed away inside. It goes without saying that this is extremely unhealthy.

I viewed the creation of a peer review process, where officers could speak confidentially with someone in the department, as an important step toward unlocking the heavily lidded box where they keep trauma from the job hidden away from others—and themselves.

The plan to upgrade the Portland Police Department operations started with adding new "hardware"—new patrol cars, radios, and emergency response vehicles. The big endeavor involved moving into the brand-new headquarters building on Middle Street. The building was much more accommodating of public access to services. There were also new offices, interrogation rooms, holding cells, and crime investigation facilities. Of major significance were the new auditorium and the opening of a gleaming new gymnasium to be used for officer fitness programs—and very importantly, for the expansion of our youth athletic league activities. The gym became an active center of interaction and engagement between officers and the city's youth.

Another change I made that didn't initially sit well with officers was my decision to hire women for the force. It was timely, but also newly required by federal law against discrimination due to race or gender. At the time, we had only one female, and she worked as a youth bureau officer—in addition to those who worked as secretaries and office support staff. The city council amended the civil service ordinance to come into compliance with federal law.

I also had the council include changes to the existing ordinance that had required female applicants to be older and have more education than their male counterparts. Changes to physical requirements were, in fact, part of a national trend that had been sparked by a case brought in Los Angeles by a woman applicant. The judgment ruled in her favor, declaring that the creation of one standard for all candidates discriminated against both women and many Asians. As a consequence, the federal government announced that it was going to withhold grant money to all police agencies where discriminatory standards remained unchanged.

The local papers made much ado about the hiring of the first two female officers. It was a mainstay, front-page story in the Portland newspapers for a while. They generally favored the move, making much of it as a "human interest" story. Ironically—a sign of the times—many of the articles referred to the two young female officers as "girls."

Some of the older officers on the force didn't like the changes that allowed women to have greater parity in hiring. They argued that it was a safety issue that they couldn't feel confident that female officers would provide the same level of backup that male officers could. This led to some initial harassment that wasn't just unseemly, but dangerous.

A situation developed where a few officers who were out on patrol began causing radio calls made by female officers to be disconnected. They did this by anonymously "clicking" their radio handsets. This prevented critical backup responses from taking place, leaving the women officers out there on their own.

When I became apprised of this, I responded without hesitation. I announced that it would stop immediately. And if it didn't, I would spend whatever money I needed to for technology that would identify which patrol cars on the streets were responsible for such activity.

This went a long way toward quelling the worst of such behavior. But it was one of the women officers out on patrol one night that made the most significant and profound change in attitudes among male counterparts.

The woman officer on patrol happened to notice movement inside of a gas station that was closed for the night. She radioed that she was going to investigate. She did. And she found an intruder inside. By the time backup arrived, she'd already cuffed and arrested the man. That incident significantly shifted attitudes and put an end to any debate whether women were up to the job.

Slowly but steadily, the Portland Police Department was changing.

CHAPTER TWENTY

Police Death Squad—And an Ending

In the summer of 1974, an extremely disturbing circumstance came to my attention. One of my shift commanders came to me with an incredible story that three of his officers had shared with him.

Apparently there had been an off-duty party that had been attended by several officers. There was drinking and carrying on, and sometime during the evening, one officer remarked to three others how the courts were too lenient, allowing people to go free who shouldn't be allowed on the streets. This officer said that they should take it upon themselves to eliminate such individuals.

At the time, the patrolmen who heard him say this thought that it was just the alcohol the patrolman had consumed that was fueling his rancor. But the next day, Officer Charles Stephens approached them again to ask whether they were with him in his plan to kill the three candidates that he'd selected because they had no value to society. When the patrolmen realized he was actually serious, two of them went to their shift commander, and he'd come to me.

I met with the department attorney, and we talked with the deputy chiefs. We called in all three patrolmen who'd reportedly heard it firsthand. They said Stephens had already picked out people he intended to eliminate. When the three asked him what would happen if other officers happened along while they were engaged in the act, Stephens said that they would just kill the other officers as well.

We also learned from one officer that he'd sat parked in a patrol car one night with Stephens and witnessed him take his gun out and aim it at various people walking down the street. Another recounted how he'd witnessed Stephens take his nightstick and batter the dash of the patrol car they were in.

They told us that Stephens had already bought a shotgun to use in the killings, because it was impossible to do ballistics if a shotgun was used. I knew we needed to move quickly. I met with the city manager and also with the head of psychiatry at Maine Medical Center.

We ended up borrowing a transmitter from the state police. The three patrolmen that Stephens had solicited ended up going out for an evening with him to discuss the details further. They drove around for a while, their conversation being taped. During their time together, Stephens showed them where they would bury the bodies at a construction site on Riverside Street on the outskirts of town. When they came back into the city, one of the officers asked to be let off, and he went to a pay phone to report that Stephens seemed ready to act soon.

There was no time to waste. We pulled together a small group of patrolmen who played baseball together in a city league. We had them put on their baseball shirts and caps to drive down to where Stephens lived in Saco. As crazy as the guy sounded, we didn't know what to expect if a contingent of cops showed up at his door, ready to arrest him.

So they went to the remote spot where Stephens lived in a trailer and went to his door, calling out for him to come out and go drinking with them, as they'd just won a ball game. When Stephens appeared, they seized him.

Stephens was taken to Maine Medical Center where he was interviewed by a psychiatrist. He denied that he was ever serious about the plan, that he meant it only "as a joke." Stephens was arrested and subsequently involuntarily committed for a three-week observation.

The Cumberland County grand jury heard the facts of the case as presented by the prosecution. The hearing, however, was disrupted when we received a bomb threat. No evidence of a bomb was found, and ultimately, the hearing was reconvened.

The officers he'd solicited testified against him. One told how Stephens planned "to remove habitual offenders because the city would be better off" without them. Another testified that Stephens had spoken to him about it while they were having beers at a bar in Saco, but that he'd not taken the plan seriously at first, "because he was intoxicated." Yet another recounted how Stephens said his plan was to help "clean up the city."

The grand jury indicted Stephens for solicitation for murder, for "wrongly and wickedly and with malice intent" conspiring to have three officers join him in killing various individuals.

At the end of his three-week involuntary commitment, however, he was released. Charles Stephens had his lawyer file a million-dollar suit claiming that his civil rights had been violated by the city.

Things got curiouser and curiouser. In early September, Governor Kenneth Curtis received a letter from Philip Shaw, who was coordinator of the New England Prisoners Association, relating how Deputy Sherriff "Bob" Hamilton told him and Russ Carmichael, who was executive director of the association, that "as a matter of fact," I was the "original planner and participant of the 'Portland Police Death Squad,' and that I had backed out only at the last minute when another original member became nervous." The "fact" of the matter, the letter claimed, was that I had developed a list of some twenty-two possible offenders living in the Portland area who needed to be eliminated.

Shaw's letter went on to say that he didn't know the veracity of the claim, but that it should be investigated and that disclosure of names on the list should be made public "so that the condemned persons will have the common sense not to stop for a Portland police cruiser pending completion of this investigation."

Though Governor Curtis certified that there was no merit to the entire claim, the accusation was part of the whole sensational atmosphere that surrounded the trial. Before it was over, my family and I received death threats. The trial, however, went forward.

The trial was conducted in Cumberland County Superior Court. A jury of seven women and five men deliberated less than two hours and found Charles Stephens, twenty-seven, guilty of "solicitation of murder" in connection with an attempt to form a death squad composed of City of Portland police officers. He was sentenced to the county jail for eleven months. He appealed and was released. The Appellate Court denied the appeal two years later, and the verdict was upheld.

Despite Portland being relatively quieter compared to Harvey and Benton Harbor, my personal response, in how it affected me, was a surprise. Our move to Portland marked the beginning of a period of great internal unease in me. I was completely caught off guard by it. Paradoxically, given the opportunity to finally spend more time with my family, I felt estranged from my wife. I felt I didn't truly know her anymore, that my years of being "absent" from the family had caused us to become strangers to one another. It wasn't that Mary or my daughters treated me any differently. It was, in a way, like I didn't know how to live with them. I felt terrible, and it caused me great emotional distress. It was a sad time. I didn't understand it, and didn't know what to do about it.

Well into the second year we were here, I came to the extremely painful decision that I needed to move out. In 1974, I found an apartment in Freeport. I spent much of my free time alone. I had earlier purchased a motorcycle and went on long rides by myself and as a part of a group of riders who frequently did weekend rides together. I tried to maintain contact with the girls, but it was awkward. They, too, couldn't make sense of what I was going through. They spent alternate holidays with me. They also sometimes dropped by the police headquarters downtown after they got out of school at Portland High at the end of the day, especially Pat. Portland High was only a few blocks away. I always made time for them. I think we were all feeling our way forward. I always enjoyed seeing them. But overall, it was a very strange and strained time for me personally.

CHAPTER TWENTY-ONE

New Tools, and Elvis and Me

We were making great strides in improving policing in Portland, but were operating in an awkward environment, where people expected more and better services while at the same time funding was being stretched. This was true on a national level. Following the riots at the Democratic Convention and the general unrest and disruptive civil disobedience around the Vietnam War, Congress passed the Omnibus Crime Control and Safe Streets Act of 1968. The legislation established the Law Enforcement Association Administration (LEAA) to administer specified policies. One policy called for the creation of state agencies to develop comprehensive plans for the improvement of law enforcement in each state.

I was chief in Benton Harbor at the time, and we benefitted greatly from the largess of the federal government. We received grant money to acquire all kinds of new hardware and equipment—with very little oversight either in the review or disbursement cycles. Police departments expanded significantly, and services were added. The public grew to expect this new level of activity and service from their local police.

The flood of money, however, was short-lived, and departments were faced with addressing the pressing issue of how to provide quality services with smaller budgets. Personally, I saw this as a great opportunity to increase efficiency and management of departments everywhere—Portland, included.

In 1975, the LEAA made a major shift in the awarding of what money it did have available to emphasize innovation over hardware. Assessing how we operated in Portland revealed that two-thirds of department resources were devoted to uniformed patrol, and that as much as 70 percent of the time that officers were out, they were nondirected in terms of central command setting priorities. We submitted a grant proposal to fund the creation of a crime analysis unit. There were numerous adjunct elements to this proposal, including most significantly the funding of a relatively new marvel, the computer, to perform rapid analysis of crime data. This was designed to aid us in better allocating resources to target areas of high crime, in terms of staffing and making assignments appropriately for every shift. Another goal was to help us implement crime prevention programs that were better targeted in the community.

Portland ended up being one of seventeen law enforcement agencies in the country to receive a grant. Ours was for $117,000.

We had already begun to compile better statistics on calls for assistance. Characteristics we tracked included time of day, nature of the incident, and the frequency of each major category of incident. With the aid of the grant money, we were able to computerize this practice by sharing available capacity on the city's central computer. Once computerized, we gained considerable visibility to what was happening in the city shift-by-shift, day-by-day. This new information was invaluable.

We also streamlined and standardized the form that officers used to report activities. We developed training to help implement this new program, with special emphasis on getting officers to use a standard terminology, which made comparative analysis more reliable.

The new system also gave us a way to assess factors that might be contributing to high rates of crime in one area of the city over another. This often entailed such factors as neighborhood bars or areas of the city where kids didn't have any organized activities to occupy their time. We had about 150 officers on the force at the time, and we wanted to use each one as effectively as possible.

This information was a great help in directing the Selective Enforcement Unit (SEU) that I'd created in my first year on the job. This unit was composed of four plainclothes officers. They were not truly an undercover unit, but were instructed to use their "wiles and guiles" to blend into the environment, with an eye to monitoring development of potential problems. They traveled the city in unmarked cars. They were encouraged to mingle and engage in open dialogue with people out on the streets to better learn what was going on. One officer, for example, gave a ride to a hitchhiker, who soon after getting in the car lit up a joint. Surprise! He ended up going to jail. In the first fifty days that the SEU was in action, it made over a hundred arrests. The new data-driven crime analysis unit helped us better pinpoint where these officers should patrol.

These initiatives greatly affected the crime rate in the city. We saw a 7 percent drop in auto theft, burglary, and robbery in 1976 alone.

I had recently completed a master's program in business administration at the University of Southern Maine. Even though I'd received a bachelor's of science at Michigan State University back in 1963, I think I still carried a sense of stigma for having flunked out from my first go-round at college. I enjoyed the program at USM, and I enjoyed being back in the stimulating environment of the classroom.

William B. McClaran

After I completed my master's, I looked into doing some part-time teaching at Southern Maine Vocational Technology Institute (SMVTI) in South Portland—what would subsequently become Southern Maine Community College (SMCC). It wasn't a surprise to me that I greatly enjoyed it. I'd always enjoyed developing and administering training programs for my officers, going back to my first position as chief in Harvey, Illinois.

I was asked by the head of the police academy in Waterville, the institute responsible for training all law enforcement officers in the state of Maine, to teach a class there. I was happy to oblige. But I wasn't prepared for the environment I found.

When I walked into class the first day, all the students rose and stood at attention. I was completely taken aback.

"Please. Sit down," I finally managed.

"Sir, yes, sir," came a ringing response as the students took their seats.

The academy was a strict, no-nonsense kind of place, more boot camp than educational in tone and practice. "Sir, yes, sir" and "Sir, no, sir" rang out through the classrooms and the hallways all day long. Despite my insistence that my students relax, that calling me "sir" was unnecessary, they would respond, "Sir, yes, sir."

The strictures of discipline were everywhere in evidence. In the dorms, students had to maintain demanding standards with regards to how their beds were made; how their clothes were folded and placed in their dressers; and how their shirts and pants were hung in the closest. A cadre, as individual instructors were called, could enter their rooms at any time to make inspection. If there wasn't a two-fingers-width spacing between each item hanging in the closest, it was common for the cadre to throw all the clothes on the floor. In moving about in the hallways, students had to always keep their gun hand free. If a cadre saw them carrying a book in that hand,

140

the offender was given demerits. While waiting in line to be served meals, students were often approached by cadres who asked them formal questions. If students didn't respond promptly with the correct answer, they were sent to the end of the line.

I was greatly distressed by all this. Despite my continued insistence that my students relax in class or when engaging me in conversation anywhere at the academy, they would always formally respond as though I were their drill sergeant.

Portland, like all other municipalities, used the academy as its main training center. The general rule in the state was that a new recruit had to attend the academy sometime before the end of his or her first year on the job. Some departments required that their recruits attend a brief pre-academy program before being formally enrolled at the state academy in Waterville. And there were some smaller departments around the state that allowed reserve patrolmen who typically worked the night shift to carry weapons and have the full duties of a regular officer with little more than a week's training. I was an anomaly in that I wouldn't allow any of my new recruits to go out on patrol until they'd been through the academy.

Not everything about the job was serious and angst ridden. I greatly enjoyed all kinds of music and many different performers, but I had a special fondness for Elvis Presley. I'd followed his career from youthful hip-swiveling performer on the *Ed Sullivan Show*, a Sunday evening TV variety show, to rising phenomenal star—singer and movie actor—to his time in the army, and to his subsequent transformation into a costumed headliner in Las Vegas.

When Elvis was scheduled to go on tour in late summer of 1977, his first stop was to be Portland, Maine. I was excited. When his advance security detail came to make arrangements, they met with me.

Being a fan, I was pleased to work with them. I knew that Elvis was a fan of local police departments and that he had a collection of ex-officio police badges given to him on his visits around the country as small honorariums. I asked if I could make a presentation to him of a Portland Police Department badge. Certainly, they said. So arrangements were made where I would meet his private plane at the Portland airport and present it to him.

I had a City of Portland badge minted especially for Elvis. It was a replica of the one I wore, but it had a pale blue center rather than a golden one. His advance team had given me complimentary tickets, and I was excited about him coming, anticipating taking Pat and Lynn to his Portland performance. Everything was set for Elvis to arrive on August 17.

On the morning of August 17, however, major news headlines across the country and around the world told that Elvis Presley had died. He'd died at Graceland, his splendorous home outside Memphis. He was only forty-two years old.

The official cause of death was listed as "cardiac arrhythmia." But this proved a cover for the real story. An autopsy showed that he'd died of a lethal cocktail of assorted drugs.

"The King" was dead. His death affected many people like the death of true royalty.

To this day, I still have the special Portland Police Department badge that I had planned to present to Elvis. It's framed and on display in my office at the community college in South Portland. I still favor listening to his early music, often playing it softly while working in my office.

CHAPTER TWENTY-TWO

The Need for Good and Decent Cops

March 8, 1976, I received a phone call from my sister, Joan. She told me that our mother was in the hospital, gravely ill. I caught the next flight out of Portland bound for Grand Rapids. I arrived March 9 and went immediately to the hospital. My sister met me and told me that our mother had passed shortly before my flight landed. We were both devastated. Mom had been through so much, but she had always been there with encouragement and support for us. We were grateful for her constancy of heart and good cheer that always brightened our lives. She was laid to rest next to our father in Grand Rapids.

That summer, my divorce was final. I married Mary Force in the fall. I had come to know her through interactions with various other departments and bureaus in the city, as she worked as an administrative assistant to a department head when I first arrived. Mary was originally from Pennsylvania, but her family moved to Maine when she was very young. She'd graduated from Bonny Eagle High School and had attended a couple of years of college before going to work for the city. She was very outgoing and upbeat, and she always lit up a room, adding a lovely spark to any group. She also had a delightful sense of humor.

After we married, we moved into her mother's house in Buxton, Maine. It was a spacious old colonial. Her mother, Evelyn Force, had decided she was ready to downsize, so she and Mary essentially swapped houses, with Evelyn moving to the house next door where Mary lived.

I'd always long thought that my position as chief of police in Portland would be yet another stepping-stone to becoming chief in a bigger city elsewhere. But after residing here a few years, I came to realize that I truly enjoyed living in Maine. It was beautiful, and the quality of life was vastly more pleasant than anywhere else I'd ever lived. We had a small boat we moored in Falmouth, and one summer, we rented a small place on an island for a week. We were the only inhabitants. And we loved it.

My first wife remarried in 1977. Bob Wolf was a Unitarian Universalist minister, and together they established a home in Falmouth. I liked Bob. I was grateful that Mary had found such a good and decent man, and in marrying him, finally achieved stable ground after moving so frequently with me. Every year the four of us, Mary and her husband, and my wife and I, along with our son, Will, and the girls, would get together during the summer at their camp on a lake near Winthrop, Maine.

When I had first arrived in the city to start as chief, two professors from the relatively new law enforcement program at the SMVTI came to introduce themselves. At the time, I didn't even know there was a college with such a program in existence. We kept in touch over the next couple of years, and I was ultimately asked to teach a few night courses in 1977. I'd done some teaching during the time I was chief in Benton Harbor. In teaching at SMVTI, I discovered I greatly enjoyed the interaction with students. They were so vibrant, so curious. Every term was different—every class was different. Different kids, different personalities, different struggles in their search to set a direction for their lives.

I decided that I wanted to settle in one place, rather than continue to move on. I applied for a full-time teaching position at SMVTI and was offered the job. I retired as chief of the Portland Police Department in the summer of 1978. Mary continued to work for the city as administrative assistant, now to the new chief of police. In the fall, I continued to teach Introduction to Law Enforcement and other classes as well.

This was a time of new ventures for me. We continued to keep a boat moored in Falmouth, and I got a license to trap lobster. It was never a serious business, but it was serious fun. We enjoyed spending as much of our free time as possible in warm weather out on Casco Bay. The next summer while we were out on the bay, we happened to strike up a conversation with an old lobsterman. We mentioned how we'd enjoyed the week we'd spent living on an island. That prompted him to mention that he knew of a small island that had recently come up for sale. Mary and I found the island on the map, located just off Bailey Island on the edge of Broad Sound. We took the boat and cruised around the island. It was only a spot in the water, about five acres, but it was lovely. We thought the idea of owning an island was pretty cool. We called the agent representing the owner, and made an offer of $20,000. The owner accepted. And we became the proud owners of Great Mark Island.

The following summer, I hired several students to help me ferry building materials over to the island. Local builders constructed a simple, very basic two-bedroom cabin. There was no electricity, no running water, and no plumbing. We had a propane gas stove and refrigerator. We collected rainwater for our use. And I hauled an outhouse out there and labored it into position behind the main house. Mary would come out to stay with me on the weekends, bringing her pack of dogs with her. She loved dogs—couldn't say no to a set of soulful eyes starting up at her through the steel lattice of an animal shelter cage. By then, her pack numbered three big dogs. And they loved staying on the island, running totally free. But there was no insulation in the place. So in the fall, when the weather started turning cooler, I'd shutter and lock it up for the winter and move permanently back home to Buxton.

One of my favorite subjects to teach was First Amendment rights. Invariably I would talk about the hippies of the 1960s and 1970s who had had such a profound impact on changing the direction of the country. I told of how one young girl walking down a sidewalk in Chicago had written "Fuck" in lipstick on her forehead. She was arrested. This, I told my students, was a clear and obvious violation of the First Amendment guarantee to free speech.

I always asked my classes whether they favored capital punishment. I'd ask for a show of hands. Routinely, a great majority of student hands would go up. Then I'd ask if there was anyone who didn't favor it. One or two hands might go up. Mine included. I told them that it had never made sense to me that a society that prohibited murder would have no qualms about killing criminals as punishment.

One of my favorite courses was one for first-year students, entitled Law of Arrest, Search, and Seizure. In essence, it was the nuts and bolts of being a cop. We would talk a lot about what proof was needed for search and seizure and for arresting someone. We would address reasonable suspicion, probable cause, when you can pull a car over, when you can search it, the evidence necessary to make an arrest, and the importance of Miranda rights.

As an example, I would ask students what they would say if they were pulled over by the cops and asked if it was okay to search their trunk. Almost invariably, everyone agreed that they'd allow the cops to conduct the search. I'd ask why. I told them that cops have to have probable cause to search a car, and lacking that, you are completely within your rights to say no. If you grant them permission, anything incriminating that they find can be used to bring charges against you.

One Monday morning soon after having this discussion with one class, a student came in to recount how he'd been pulled over on Friday night in Portland, and the officers had wanted to search his car. He asked them if they had probable cause. The officers were taken aback. Flustered, they eyed one another—then they told him to take off.

We talked about when you can frisk someone. When I was a beat patrolman, when I had probable cause, I would search for weapons—guns or knives. But I said it is much more challenging today. Weapons can look like a pager or a cell phone. You have to take a careful look to make sure that common, ordinary things aren't some kind of weapon. Or a device for hiding drugs—like a cell phone, where violators sometimes hide their drugs in the battery compartment.

I routinely tracked several publications reporting on criminal trials so that I could keep abreast of court interpretations of the law. There was one case where an officer had taken a police dog to make an inquiry at a house. The dog, trained to detect drugs, "alerted" the officer. The officers went ahead and obtained a search warrant and found drugs on the premises. The trial, however, turned on whether the handler had had probable cause to bring the animal to the front door of the house in the first place. The court ruled that he did not, and the case was dismissed.

You have to be careful, also, about the vagueness of requirements regarding some actions. One case I told my students about was in Michigan, and it was really perplexing. There was a requirement that you had to "knock and announce" your presence when you go to search a residence, unless you have a "no knock" warrant, used in instances where it might be a danger to knock. You're supposed to give residents a "reasonable time" to open the door. In the case in Michigan, the officers knocked and announced—and immediately kicked the door open. The officers found drugs, and the occupant was arrested. The defendant's lawyer filed a motion that the case be dismissed due to failure to provide a reasonable time between knocking and forcefully entering the residence. The court ruled that it was not going to dismiss the case, thereby allowing the evidence to be entered, rather than ruling it inadmissible. The court, however, also declared that the defendant could file a civil suit, claiming that his right of protection against unlawful search and seizure had been violated. This despite the fact that defendant was going to jail.

Justice? Perhaps. But the ruling mostly served only to muddy already murky waters.

I often used videos in class. One I often showed was on the use of force. Police use of force has becoming increasingly challenged in court. (Today I tell my students that you always should assume that you're being filmed—either by cameras that have become common in patrol cars, or by bystanders, visible or not, using smartphones.) The important point was that officers have to be extremely cognizant about the use of force. They aren't permitted—and can't allow themselves—to feel above the law in meting out force. Constitutional law mandates restraint. These constitutional rights serve and protect everyone—including law enforcement personnel. These rights are truly the foundation of a civil society.

———

I typically asked students in my first-year introduction class on law enforcement how many had family members or knew people in law enforcement. I routinely got a show of hands. I asked how many had definitely decided on a career in law enforcement. The number of hands varied, but there were usually at least three or four.

I followed this by warmly inviting them all to join me in the law enforcement field. I told them if you became an officer you would probably work nights and weekends. And Thanksgiving and Christmas. Your circle of friends would mostly be composed of other cops. If you made a career of it, you'd be more likely than the general population to experience serious stress on the job; more likely to use alcohol excessively; and suffer more divorce, heart attacks, and suicide than the general population. It was always a sobering moment. But I wanted my students to fully know what they were getting into. It's a great and rewarding career, but it can also be isolating, lonely, and not conducive to your mental and physical health.

Being a cop, in my book, is not just about catching the bad guys. It's a public service. There have been changes toward a more open embrace of community policing, but old behaviors die hard. If my students are truly interested in public service, I encourage them to consider going into law enforcement. The field needs all the good and decent people it can get.

CHAPTER TWENTY-THREE

A Hard Look at Police Training

Training was always a top priority in all my administrations as chief of police, from Harvey to Portland. It paralleled my belief that the duty of a police officer is first and foremost to be a public servant, and that most people warranted being treated with the utmost respect.   From my experience and observations, however, these views were not universal throughout all police and law enforcement agencies in the United States.

So, in 1985, while on the faculty at SMVTI, I decided to get a PhD. I selected as my dissertation topic a comparative study of police training in Maine and in the British Isles. I elected to study Britain and Ireland, as I had observed community policing there as being the very best in the world, characterized by a completely different mind-set and form of engagement and interaction of police with locals. The college was generous in granting me a semester sabbatical to do field research.

I'll never forget my first day at the London Metropolitan Police training facility, known as the Peel Center, one of England's national police training centers located outside London. As I was introduced around, people kept remarking that "training must be so fabulous in America—so much better than here." This attitude of deference to the United States surprised me. I'd smile and remark that it was one of the things I certainly wanted to investigate, that is, how exemplary, or not, our training was in the United States. I was asked if cops were armed like in the then-popular television program *Hill Street Blues*. I told them that some license was taken with American television shows and movies, but that the violence and preoccupation with guns were, in fact, realities. I learned that only 10 percent of the police in England are armed, primarily department detectives. The general feeling was that a gun was a kind of "crutch" that got in the way of good community policing.

I was welcomed everywhere I went. Over the course of three months, I visited the Peel Center several times, and also Scotland Yard. I also spent time in Ireland studying its national training academy.

Because police training and assignment in England and Ireland are organized on a national level, instruction is based on a single, universal set of principles and practices; once candidates successfully complete the training, they can seek assignment anywhere in the country.

The English training system requires five months of training before a cadet can be assigned to patrol the streets. In comparison, I came to feel that training in Maine was almost an afterthought. I ended up finding far more contrasts between the two systems than similarities. The sharp points of contrast, I would ultimately surmise, have a huge impact on the style of interaction between police and citizens in England and Ireland, and also that in America.

An anecdote I was told while at the Peel Center aptly characterized the stark differences. An officer told me of an encounter he had while traveling to New York City on vacation.

The first thing that the officer noticed was all the equipment and gear that New York cops carried, much of it hanging from their belts. This included a gun, a nightstick, handcuffs, ammunition, and

Mace—just to start. Looking for his hotel, the London officer went up to a New York cop on the street to ask directions.

"He wheeled around like a carousel, with all the stuff on his belt flying as he turned. The guy told me, 'Whatta you think I am, buddy? A tour guide or somethin'?'"

I decided to do a comparative test while I was in London. I went up to an unarmed bobby near Trafalgar Square to ask him how I could find the square. The officer smiled and said, "How fortunate you are. You're already here."

The early English policing model served as the genesis of organizations that were formed in cities in the early days of the United States. English training methods, philosophy, and course content were designed to nurture the premise that public acceptance of the mission of police is anchored in mutual respect. It should not be surprising that the early police organization in the colonies mirrored what existed in England.

The tradition of mutual, local associations having responsibility for maintaining the peace in Britain dates back to the ninth century. In time, collectives of local associations became overseen by a constable appointed by an area nobleman. These collectives were subsequently organized into shires, the equivalent of counties, and a kind of sheriff was given the task of overseeing these entities. In the fourteenth century, England created the office of the justice of the peace, where this officer assisted the sheriff in policing individual shires. Eventually, what had started as "mutual pledge" associations composed of local citizens to police themselves gave way to the hiring of others to be chartered with the responsibility for individual "watches."

The industrial revolution in England in the 1700s brought great changes to large cities like London. Slums and poverty became prevalent, and crime, juvenile delinquency, and bank robberies became commonplace. Vigilantism arose in this atmosphere, until reforms were initiated in the 1820s. The crown appointed Sir Robert Peel as home secretary. He established daytime patrols, but because of widespread mistrust among citizens, it took him seven years to get the Metropolitan Police Act approved in 1829. This central, unified authority did away with the proliferation of multiple private police groups formed by merchants, shippers, and businessmen, each narrowly focusing on its own areas of commerce. Peel immediately set about establishing a national standard training program because he understood that unregulated police behavior only added to social unrest.

"No quality is more indispensible to a police officer than perfect command of temper; a quiet determined manner has more effect than violent actions," he wrote. "The securing and training of proper persons is at the root of efficiency."

Over twelve thousand people applied for positions on the new Metropolitan Police force. They had to be under thirty-five, physically strong, and in good health; in addition, they had to be at least five feet seven inches tall and able to read and write, and they had to submit a written recommendation attesting to their good character. Only a thousand met those standards. The officers were armed only with a truncheon. And constables, as they were called, became commonly known as "bobbies"—in honor of Robert Peel.

In the mid-1800s, New York City was said to be the most crime-ridden city in the world, with Philadelphia, Baltimore, and Cincinnati not far behind. Lack of respect for police was widespread, fostered by widespread police corruption and the lack of professionalism. New York City was the first American city to create a uniformed police force, patterned after Peel's London Metropolitan Police.

As the American frontier moved westward, the model of policing became heavily weighted in favor of the appointment of sheriffs as towns sprung up, augmented in some places, especially sparsely populated areas, by state units, such as the Texas Rangers. With the shift westward, the suspicion of a distant central authority (in large part a contributing factor in sparking the American Revolution) increasingly became a characteristic of the American psyche. Citizens of the West became much more attached to guns and the notion of protecting themselves. The idea of a central system of authority for universally certifying the practices and behaviors of local authority came to be viewed as going against the emerging national grain. Arming oneself, whether one was a citizen or a local sheriff, became the norm. This became deeply ingrained in the character of the country, setting the stage for the arming of all law enforcement personnel. This was—and is—in marked contrast to law enforcement in both England and Ireland.

Today, it is understood that there are four primary methods to obtain public compliance with police directives. These four methods are:

- *Authority*—which is the most powerful, stable, and socially acceptable, with citizens having the common recognition that they should comply.
- *Power*—which is based on the acknowledgment that the enforcement system of prosecutors, courts, and sanctions present risks worthy of compelling compliance.

- *Persuasion*—which includes the use of argument and threats to overcome resistance.
- *Force*—which is the most extreme form, ranging from restraint to the taking of life.

The sources for the first two are "institutional" in nature, whereas the latter two are based on personal discretion.

Peel understood that citizens had to accept the legitimacy of police authority and power. In the United States today, police authority has generally evolved to rely predominantly on persuasion and force. The effect of this has been that personal discretion in decision making has been driven to the lowest level—down to the individual officer and his or her personal style. Armed with guns, ammunition, nightstick, handcuffs, Tasers, and Mace, the prevalent impression is that officers are prepared to use force to obtain compliance as swiftly as possible. Americans view police as being "frontline soldiers" in a war on crime. (This idea of compliance being a war on crime was christened by President Richard Nixon's War on Crime Act, passed in 1973, at the height of civil disobedience and Vietnam antiwar protests. The idea of authoritative "war" in society has also been perpetuated to this day by Nixon's lingering "war on drugs." Neither offensive has proven very effective in terms of achieving desired results. Now we also have the "war on terror." The use of such terminology erodes clear-minded thinking on means and ends, which can result in the erosion of constitutional rights.)

This type of mind-set continues to greatly affect the training of American police.

At the time I conducted my study, the contrast in training styles on either side of the Atlantic could not have been starker.

In England, recruits had to complete twenty weeks of training before being granted the full authority of an officer. There were eight individual group classes every year, composed of 160 recruits each, with over 1,200 recruits trained annually. The academy was routinely staffed by 120 officers of various ranks, including six chief inspectors, two superintendents, and one commander.

Physical training was emphasized, ranging from swimming to defensive tactics. The academy believed that physical training builds confidence among officers who work without guns. Recruits could obtain special tutoring and support as necessary. The training program dropout rate was less than 2 percent.

The curriculum was always undergoing reassessment. Riots in London in the early 1980s led to a revamping of the program. There had been a huge influx of West Indians in England, and it was felt that officers were seriously unprepared to deal with diverse multicultural issues. As a result, a quarter of the curriculum came to focus on cultural diversity, communications, and updated community policing techniques. A two-week course was developed and required of all officers up to the level of inspectors. The emphasis in this training was on self-awareness, interpersonal skills, race, and community relations.

One of the things that greatly struck me was the atmosphere that characterized all training. The general tone was relaxed, which helped foster greater group participation. There was a great emphasis on the idea that the primary function of a police officer was to provide social services in the broadest sense of the term, ranging from arresting a burglar to stoking the furnace of an elderly citizen. Officers were encouraged first and foremost to use their intelligence and to consider the longer-term impacts of what they did.

One telling example was the story of an arresting officer who confronted a man armed with a machete standing outside of a pub.

The man was threatening to go after another man with the weapon, and he stubbornly resisted surrendering it to an officer. The officer engaged the man, trying to get him to give up the machete before the officer took him to the station. The two finally settled on the offender giving up his machete—but as an accommodating compromise, he was allowed to drive himself to the station.

In the United States at the time, a national survey of occupational prestige revealed that police ranked forty-seventh out of fifty occupations, falling below undertakers and agricultural workers. Here in this country, police were viewed as the government's most visible symbol of official limitations imposed on citizens. There was also a widespread distrust of central authority, which led to wide disparity in police training.

The US President's Commission on Law Enforcement and Administration of Justice, created in the 1960s after the social unrest of the times, issued a report in 1967 entitled "The Challenge of Crime in a Free Society." The report stated that police recruit training "should consist of an absolute minimum of 400 hours of classroom work, spread over a few to six-month period so that it can be combined with carefully selected and supervised field training."

In 1970, a quarter of all cities and half of all small towns did nothing to train new recruits, other than referring them to the Ten Commandments. The overwhelming majority of departments that did do training put new officers on the job immediately and then trained them sometime within the first year. Most state police, as a rule, got more training than local police. Only 10 percent of states required training before a recruit assumed full police duties.

According to one study, in those states that mandated academics as part of the training curriculum, less than 8 percent of the time was devoted to aspects of human relation issues. The state of Missouri at the time required only three hours.

In Maine, with few exceptions when I was conducting my research, municipalities and counties permitted recruits to work as fully authorized officers of the law for up to nine months without first going through the academy, given that they attended a "pre-training" course.

The majority of the instructors at the Maine academy were scheduled on an ad hoc, nonpayment basis, mainly drawn from state law enforcement agencies. Other instructors included non-sworn personnel, such as lawyers, psychiatrists, and various guest lecturers. Most instructors received a one-week instructional methods course.

Of the 342 required hours of training for municipal and county officers, only eighteen hours (4 percent) were dedicated to human behavior and communication skills (in London, it was 25 percent).

The code of conduct while at the academy required unquestioned obedience to the directives of instructors. The atmosphere was highly structured and regimented, with rigid control mirroring military training. Among the regulations cadets had to adhere to were asking permission to go to the bathroom, bracing at attention when addressing staff and visitors, and not speaking unless given permission.

Where there was about a 2 percent dropout rate in the British training system, in Maine at the time, the dropout rate among municipal recruits in the first two weeks was 5 to 10 percent; among state police recruits, the dropout rate was 20 percent.

I called the academy director and asked if I could interview a cadet. The academy administration seemed very reluctant to permit this, but finally approved my speaking with one county deputy who'd been a former student of mine at SMVTI. We met in the library. Though we knew each other personally, he was very formal, and despite my persistence that he call me Bill rather than Sir, he refused. He was very nervous during the whole time we spoke together and was extremely circumspect in answering my questions.

I comment in my doctoral thesis that the "training of new police officers has great potential for positive or negative effects on the recruit, as well as the public he or she is sworn to serve. To adapt to a training style and not periodically question its appropriateness is, at best, shortsighted, and not in the best interest of the police officer nor the public." When police are trained by a military boot-camp model, what you produce are militaristically oriented "frontline soldiers."

I was never asked back to the academy. Some while later, after the recruit I'd interviewed for my thesis had graduated, I happened to run into him in public. I asked him what the deal was with how weirdly he'd acted that afternoon in the academy library. He admitted that he felt that our conversation was surreptitiously being recorded.

The year after I completed my dissertation, I testified before the state legislature about a new training bill that was under consideration. I spoke out against it. The original bill was for a twelve-week, 480-hour training course. But the police chiefs association opposed it as too burdensome and had put forward an alternative bill specifying a one-hundred-hour course.

In several municipalities, including Portland, South Portland, Falmouth, and Westbrook, the training requirement was already 480 hours.

"It doesn't go far enough," I testified of the one-hundred-hour proposal. "It leaves holes, leaving officers facing legal and physical risks. Our cops deserve more."

CHAPTER TWENTY-FOUR

Opening the World to Students

My wife, Mary, took a leave of absence from her job with the Portland Police Department so that she could accompany me on my sabbatical in Ireland. When I finished my research, we decided to stay for a time. County Kerry, and especially the Dingle Peninsula in the southwestern corner of the Emerald Isle, had become a favorite place that we loved to visit. We intended to stay for several weeks, but midway through, she started feeling ill, and we decided to return to Maine. Soon after returning, she went to see her doctor. The doctor did several tests. The diagnosis: Mary was pregnant.

Our son, William, was born in Portland on June 18, 1986, and came home with us to Buxton. I was at a very different point in my life, and I saw his birth as an opportunity to strive to be a very different kind of father.

We sold Great Mark Island, and when Will was two, we bought a very simple, two-bedroom cottage on Card Cove on the Harpswell peninsula below the city of Brunswick. It was beautiful there, and the people were friendly and welcoming. Over time, we built up and around the original structure to make a five-bedroom, two-bath, all-season home. Mary's mother came to live with us in the apartment we finished for her over the two-car garage. We had a dock where we could keep the boat and plenty of room for the dogs.

That year I was interviewed for a story in the *Maine Sunday Telegram* about older dads raising young children. Reflecting back to when we first learned that Mary was pregnant, I was quoted as saying, "I wondered what kind of father will I be when I'm older? Will I be able to play ball if it's a son?" I knew it would be different from when the girls were first born. "I was preoccupied much of the time. I was going to school and holding jobs. There were all kinds of competing interests." I went on to say, "Now, I am not in a career frenzy. I have a job that affords me considerable time off to be with my family."

Mary and I commuted from Harpswell to work in Portland. Mary's mother, Evelyn, was very helpful in looking after Will. They became very close. Will took after her in many ways, especially her interests in sports. When Evelyn was young and in school, she was a four-sport athlete. She was quite a good basketball player, back in the day when girls wore skirted uniforms. Will took a keen interest in the sport, and I put a hoop up for him in the driveway. I'd often go out when he was practicing and shoot with him.

It was very different being a dad the second time around. I was more present and involved, as I was no longer consumed 24-7 by my job.

I still greatly enjoyed working. Though I enjoyed the free time during the summers to be with my family, I always looked forward to the school year starting again in the fall. I missed being in the classroom, around students, and involved in their lives.

I was informal in interactions with my students. I told them to call me Bill. I maintained an open door policy in my office, encouraging students to come by anytime, to talk about anything, not just the material that we were covering in class. I emphasized to my students to come see me if they were ever in a pressing situation where they needed legal counsel. I said I had several friends who were lawyers who would be happy to talk to them and provide legal advice at little or no cost.

Students trusted me. They came to me to talk about struggles at home, on the job, with their friends. Many, being first in their families to go to college, worried about whether they were good enough to succeed in class. They worried about their studies, about sometimes having to miss classes because they had to work to pay expenses. On occasion, I was the first person to whom they told of extremely distressing situations, such as a death in the family or spousal abuse. In the latter case, I would arrange for them to see a counselor, and if they elected, I helped arrange their move to a protective environment.

Talking with students was one of the things I most enjoyed about the job. I always listened, gave counsel, and told them that I would do whatever was possible to help them find resolution to their situations, including finding psychological and legal help. I saw it as part of my job. Teaching to me was similar to being a police officer—it was an entrusted public service. I took great personal satisfaction from helping guide students through the process of finding themselves, and finding their way in the world. It was a thrill to watch them grow and change.

And it was also a thrill to see the college grow and change over the time I've been there. In 1989, its name was changed to Southern Maine Technical College (SMTC); then in 2003, it became Southern Maine Community College (SMCC). When I started teaching, there were only nine hundred students; today there are over seven thousand.

———

I loved to travel—and had traveled, perhaps not widely, but certainly extensively, mostly returning again and again to Ireland where I'd made many friends over the years. I knew and appreciated the value of traveling beyond what was familiar and seeing how other people lived—appreciating both the similarities and the differences. In 1988, I went to the college administration with a proposal to create and run a kind of study-abroad program within the criminal justice department. I proposed that the school permit me to take students to England over spring break to immerse them in the culture and to expose them to community policing at its best. The college agreed.

I promoted the unique opportunity to students in my classes and was very pleased to have a score or so sign up that first year. Students who went were amazed by the experience, so much so that they came back and talked it up among their friends. The program became a huge hit. Every year there was a lot of anticipation about the annual trip. I regularly started taking twenty to thirty students—sometimes as many as forty—for nine days every March. The trip was also open to anyone else who wanted to go, dependent on space availability, and occasionally our groups included other faculty and friends. Working through a friend at a travel agency, I was able to keep the cost very affordable. (Today the cost is still less than $2,000. That covers airfare, transportation, meals, and lodging for nine days.) Students were required to take a preparatory course, and then after going, to write a paper about their experience in order to receive social science or criminal justice credit toward fulfilling their requirements for graduation.

Many of my students had never been very far from home, some never outside of Maine—let alone outside the country. A good number of my students every year were from rural Maine. Some were the first in their families to go to college. Others had never flown. Such a trip was commonly viewed as the biggest adventure of their lives—sparking the desire to travel more, to see more, and to learn more about a world that they'd never truly imagined existing, a world they discovered was accessible and welcoming. One of the great learning moments for my criminal justice students was seeing that police officers there are armed only with clubs. Many found it incredible. "They don't have guns? How's that work?" There was nothing like seeing it for oneself.

The first four or five years, we partnered with the Peel Center outside of London, where people there greatly welcomed the program. Following that, I started scheduling the trip to Ireland. I, myself, was so taken by the Irish that I wanted to share the amazing hospitality and warmth of the people, the beauty of the countryside, and the richness of the island's history.

Time in Ireland was spent largely in County Kerry, with Killarney as our base. The southwestern corner of Ireland was one of the most popular destinations in all of Ireland for its spectacular natural beauty, including its rugged coastline, verdant farmlands, and beautiful mountains—County Kerry being the most mountainous region in all of Ireland. The day trip to Dingle Peninsula, which juts forty miles out into the Atlantic, was a favorite destination among the students. We also visited Ross Castle, the ancestral home of the O'Donoughue clan built in the fifteenth century, and stone beehive huts that were built before the Christian era. In addition, we always visited Blarney Castle, where students could kiss the Blarney Stone, if they were so inclined, and we visited the majestic Killarney lakes.

Of course, the major focus of the trip was to spend time learn-
_____ how the Irish train their police at its residential training
_____ cadets attend classes on campus for six months and
_____ ed to go into the field with regular officers on patrol.
_____ cadets were required to take eighteen months of train-
_____ coming fully certified.

The students also visited the Killarney Garda Station (as police stations are called in Ireland). The Killarney police were very proud of their collection of Portland Police Department patches that I had given to them over the years, displaying them prominently about the station. The visit included a full tour, including being allowed to enter its old, stone cellblock.

There was also opportunity in the evenings to visit local pubs and listen to stellar Irish pub bands. There, students got to meet other students from all over the world who came to Ireland during spring break. Such experiences profoundly affected my students' views of the world, expanding their perspectives, opening them to the idea that the world can be very different from Maine. Evenings out also frequently afforded opportunities to see local police interacting with citizens, observing how they dealt with potentially contentious situations armed only with a nightstick.

One night a group of us was outside of a pub chatting with an officer on foot patrol. She was very solicitous of the students' questions. At one point, however, she noticed an inebriated man across the street who was arguing with his wife. The officer kept talking with us, but she also kept her eye on the situation. At one point, when it looked to be turning into something more than an angry argument, she smiled at us all.

"You'll excuse, won't you? There's a situation over there that I need to attend to." We stood and watched her cross over to engage with the distraught couple. The couple quieted down, and after a couple of minutes, they turned and started walking home.

Quite commonly, students told me that the trip to Ireland was the best experience they've ever had. It was clear that it could be life transforming. Many promised to—and many did—go back again, and go on to travel more widely. They came away more confident in being able to navigate their lives and their places in the world.

I often received letters from students following the trip, telling me how unique the opportunity was, how much it moved them.

"Ireland moved me in so many ways," wrote one female student. "Thank you for sharing your experience both professionally and personally with your students (I wanted to sit and share a pint with you—and we did)."

Another wrote to say, "I hold you in my highest regards because you are not only my teacher, but my friend...[When I started school] I was scared and shy and didn't have the slightest idea what I was supposed to be doing at college. You helped guide me...with my studies, my future plans...[and] even my personal life...You have taught me so much, not only about the law—but about myself."

And another wrote, "You've not only taught me a lot about being a law enforcement officer, you've taught me a lot about being a person."

CHAPTER TWENTY-FIVE

My Mary

Mary and I both loved Ireland. My great-grandfather's people were from Northern Ireland, in County Antrim. We, however, favored southern Ireland, especially County Kerry. In time, Mary came to claim that she, too, was Irish, she was so smitten with the place and its people. I was amused at this. I did a little research to bolster my notion that she most likely came from English stock. I teased her about it, but she was not amused. Despite the long-standing, historic animosities between the Irish and the English, the Irish are generous, welcoming people, and in the eyes of our Irish friends, Mary was every bit as Irish as she wanted to be. It was the people and their way of life that drew us both, along with the incredible beauty of Ireland. We both were smitten, so such so that we started talking about moving there permanently after we retired.

During one family trip with Will in the mid-1990s, we visited a development outside of the village of Killarney where ground had just been broken for a small community of timeshare houses. We were quite taken with the plans and the model unit. All houses were to have thatched roofs. Mary and I ended up buying into a three-bedroom unit that was, at the time, little more than a foundation. When it was finished, it became a frequent destination for us—for Mary, Will, and me, where every year we made time to go to Ireland.

Will went to elementary school in Harpswell, then middle school, and the start of his freshman year in Topsham. Just before basketball season, he transferred to Pine Tree Academy in Freeport. He was a good student, but his passion was basketball. He was a starting player on the school team. Though the academy had a residential component, Will continued to live at home with us. He graduated in June 2004. That fall he entered Nichols College in Dudley, Massachusetts, attending on an academic scholarship. He tried out for the team but injured his leg, ending his play. He majored in sports management. By that time, Mary's mother, Evelyn, had passed away, and Mary and I sold our house in Harpswell and moved into Portland.

On December 29, 2005, my sister, Joan, passed. I flew to Grand Rapids for the funeral, and met her son, Scott, at the funeral home. She'd been ill for some time, but it was still a sad occasion for family and friends. Afterward, I spent time with his family, and then I flew back to Portland.

In the spring of 2008, Mary started to complain about not feeling well. Finally, in May, I got her to agree to see a doctor. I took her to Maine Medical Center. This was the day before Will was scheduled to graduate from Nichols. Pat and Lynn and their families were all going to be there. The primary physician ordered an MRI. We waited for the results. The lab technician finally came out and told us that we needed to go back and see the primary physician again. The doctor called us into his office and said he had bad news. Mary had lung cancer—and it was fairly well advanced.

We went as planned to Will's graduation. We didn't say anything, as it was Will's special day and we did not want to divert any of the attention he so richly deserved. But inside, we both were in agony.

She grew progressively worse. She started a round of chemother-apy that ran through most of the summer. Following that series, the diagnosis was that the chemo seemed to be working. By fall, it was apparent that it was not.

Mary wanted to go to Ireland. So in October, I took a week off from school, and she, Carole Ann Dunphe, her best friend, and I went to Killarney and stayed in our place for a week. Mary knew it would be her last trip.

She was in and out of the hospital throughout November. In December, she was admitted to a hospice center down in Scarborough. She spent Christmas there. And then New Year's. Will was then doing PR for the Hornets, the New Orleans NBA team, after spending six months with the Knicks in New York City. But he came home for two weeks to be with his mother. On January 3, Mary died. She was only sixty-two years old. She had long planned to retire later that year.

Her ashes were buried in Portland's Evergreen Cemetery. That summer, Will and I made a quick trip together to Killarney. He'd just moved home from New Orleans, and I was in London, but we met in Ireland. We stayed at the timeshare and made a journey out to the Dingle Peninsula, to Coomenoole Beach, one of Mary's most favorite places in all of Ireland. It wasn't a big beach, but it was beautiful, held by barren headlands, with dramatic views, there on the southwestern tip of the peninsula, staring into the broad face of the Atlantic. Mary and I had spent many hours there. Some days in late afternoon, when the weather was bright, the big breakers rolling in had a translucent quality as they crested, with the sunlight coming soft through the topmost curls, giving them a muted, blue-green sheen like sea glass. It was where scenes from the David Lean's Oscar-winning movie, *Ryan's Daughter*, were filmed. It was a place filled with memories of her.

The day Will and I went to Coomenoole, it was overcast and windy. There, we scattered the last of Mary's ashes, a small portion that we'd kept aside so that we could bring them there. In our many years coming there together as a family, Mary had, indeed, truly become part Irish. And now, as well, she had become a very real part of Ireland.

CHAPTER TWENTY-SIX

The Grace of Second Chances

It was a difficult adjustment to a life without Mary. She had made me wondrously happy for over thirty years. Her bright smile, her easy laugh, her rich sense of humor. I was fortunate, however, to have my teaching. It was a godsend, really, being around my students. So much potential, so much ahead of them—tempered always with their search to find their way and their places in the world. Being a part of that had been—and continues to be—like a deep keel that steadied me. They gave me much, and I was grateful. And I was also grateful for my children, my two daughters, Pat and Lynn and their families, and for my son, Will.

In the summer of 2011, a little over two years after Mary died, I invited Pat and Lynn and their husbands, Michael and Kevin, and Will and his girlfriend to join me on a trip to Ireland. The trip was my gift to them. Everyone was able to go, including Lynn's two children, her daughter, Erin, and her son, Michael. But Pat's son, Patrick, was unable to join us, as he'd just started a new job. In June, we flew to Shannon and spent two wonderful weeks together.

I had always greatly enjoyed the trips with students, showing them all the places I loved, exposing them to the incredible beauty of Ireland and of its people. And finally, on the trip with my children and their families, I got to do the same with them. It was a fabulous trip.

The following summer, I took my daughters and their husbands to London. We saw all the sights—Buckingham Palace, the Tower of London, and Madame Tussauds, and we also went to the theater. After they left, I flew on to Ireland to spend two weeks by myself. I came back and started another year at SMCC.

By late September, I had started to not feel well. In early October, I went to the doctor. After examining me, he immediately admitted me for open-heart surgery. Pat and Lynn each came for extended stays to attend to my recovery. Mary's death and then my surgery were sobering. They caused me to reflect on many things—things I had missed out on, things I had wished I'd done differently, and also on things that I was deeply grateful for. On this last point, top of the list were my children.

Around Christmastime, I began thinking about taking my daughters and their husbands back to Ireland. We discussed it. And they discussed it with their husbands. It didn't look likely. Michael, Pat's husband, felt that he needed to visit his father the coming summer in Minnesota. Kevin, Lynn's husband, couldn't spare the time off. I was disappointed.

And then Lynn, after talking to her sister, called to suggest that just the three of us go. We'd never before done anything like it. I thought it was a wonderful idea. And so I set about planning the trip and making arrangements for us to go in June, after the college term ended.

In the weeks leading up to our departure, it was obvious in our phone conversations that we were all growing very excited. "I can't wait," Pat was fond of saying. Lynn kept remarking how it would be such a great opportunity for the three of us to "bond" together. The idea of the three of us together in Ireland for ten days made me almost giddy.

As it worked out, after the term ended, I flew to London with three friends for five days. Like the earlier trip there with my daughters and their families, I loved showing my friends the sights. We, too, went to the Tower of London, to Buckingham Palace, had a cruise on the Thames, and went to the theater. After nearly a week, we flew to Ireland, and again I delighted in showing them the Ireland that I loved. After this leg of the trip, I dropped them off at the airport so that they could fly back to Maine.

The morning my daughters were to arrive, I got up well before dawn to make the drive to Shannon in County Clare to meet them at the airport. The two of them had met the night before in Boston, and were flying over together.

I'm an extremely punctual person. I arrived at baggage claim before their flight was due in—but their flight had been early and they were already there. They took great delight in my "being late." We drove back to Killarney and had a quiet day, as they were both tired from the long night flight from the States. We went out to O'Donoughue's Pub in Killarney for dinner and to listen to music. We were all in great spirits, finally being together again in Ireland— just the three of us.

We settled into a comfortable routine. During the day, we went out in the mornings and afternoons to see various sights and to revisit favorite places each had wanted to see again. Then in the evening, we'd go out early for dinner and to listen to live music at a couple of my favorite pubs.

Early in our stay, they wanted to go to Adrigole, a small village down on the Beara Peninsula, one of the major peninsulas that give shape to the southwestern corner of Ireland. A small gift shop in

Adrigole was known for its beautiful, one-of-a-kind works of art. The owner is a friend of actor Colin Farrell, and had taught him how to play the guitar when he was young.

We also spent time visiting sites in the Ring of Kerry, seeing Ross Castle, Loch Leane, and Ladies View—a spectacular panoramic overview, all in the National Park near Killarney, a magical 23,000-acre preserve. One day we drove up to Moll's Gap, where we had coffee and could look out over the surrounding mountains. We also visited the Muckross House, a neo-Gothic mansion favored by Queen Victoria during her visit to Ireland in the 1860s; and also the village of Kenmare, a community founded in the seventeenth century and known today for its numerous, fine shops.

We went one day to Glengarriff for lunch. Glengarriff was at the head of the Beara Peninsula, on Bantry Bay. It was situated such that the Gulf Stream made it a temperate garden spot, covered with lush vegetation. We made the long drive to Healy Pass, up the narrow, one-lane road to the summit. The road was so narrow that buses and large trucks are not permitted; when two vehicles meet, considerable thought had to be given to how to get around one another. It was one of Lynn's favorite spots to have our picture taken. We stopped at the small seasonal store there so that we could all get a Magnum ice cream bar, one of my favorite treats.

One day we visited Sneem, a unique little village that sits astride a river. It was beautiful and charming, with numerous modern, outdoor sculptures. We went into the pharmacy there to get something. And the pharmacist remembered me from an earlier visit some years before.

"You were in here with a hand. How is it?" he asked.

I was amazed that he remembered me. I'd gone into to get bandages for a cut on my hand, and the pharmacist had sat me down and bandaged it himself. "That should take care of it," he'd told me at the time. I told him that my hand was quite fine, thank you. The small encounter was an example among countless others of the warmth and generosity of spirit of the Irish people.

Another favorite place for both girls was Moriarty's Store, which was located near the Gap of Dunloe. It was a very high-end store, selling clothes, jewelry, crystal, and fine pottery. Of course Lynn enjoyed dropping by, as Moriarty is her married name. We also stopped in at Mulcahy's in Ballyferriter, which showcases some of the finest pottery in all of Ireland. It was always one of Mary's favorite places. The day we went, I had each of my daughters pick something special to commemorate our trip together.

We drove around the entire Dingle Peninsula. The road was extremely narrow, with numerous roundabouts. Pat and Lynn squabbled over who had to sit in front with me. They claimed I drove like a maniac. Drivers in Ireland sit on the right side of the car, as they do in England. I was quite comfortable with it at this point, having driven countless miles sitting to the right. But the road was indeed very narrow, with tight twists and turns following the crenelated coastline. It took a brave heart for many a tourist to sit on the left without the security of a steering wheel.

One of the places we stopped was Coomenoole Beach, out at the tip of the Dingle Peninsula. There were many places in Ireland that hold deep, powerful memories of my Mary, but this was perhaps the most stirring. It was where Will and I had scattered a portion of her ashes. It always made me miss her—remembering all the great times we had together. It meant much to me that the girls went with me that day to stand again on the beach that Mary loved.

We went out every night to one or the other of my favorite pubs around Killarney. Four different nights we went to O'Donoughue's

Pub, where the group Tintean played. It was perhaps my favorite pub, and I'd designated a table down near the band as my "personal" table. I always tried to make a point of getting there early for dinner before the music started so that I could claim it. One night, the table was already occupied. I glowered at the party at the table, but they didn't seem to take any note of me. My daughters tried to get to me let it go, but I wouldn't. I made us shift three times from table to table, drawing closer, until the party finally finished for the evening and left. My daughters were both amused and embarrassed, but they know me well enough to know that once I have a plan, nothing will shake me from it. It was a tradition for me, as I've never failed to sit at "my" table.

The music and the food were fabulous. I always got the seafood chowder—which never failed to satisfy. The group was known for their jigs. In the middle of one set, an eighty-year-old woman got up and started step dancing. The band, the crowd, my daughters, and I loved it.

We also went to Molly Darcy's, one of my other favorite pubs, where the band Anora played. Anora was a fabulous Irish group. It changed a bit in makeup over time, but was essentially composed of the three O'Connor brothers—Patrick, Brendan, and Anthony. Helena Connelly, who had a beautiful voice, sang with them when we were there. At one point, Anthony looked out and noticed me sitting at my favorite table.

"Aye, look who's here? We have Bill McClaran from the States. I say, Bill, are those two lovely ladies your dates?" I smiled and said they were my daughters. "Aye. And as a special feature tonight, Bill's going to sing with us," he announced.

My daughters turned to me in amazement. "Are you really going to sing?"

"Well, I'm going to sing *along*," I replied. And like everyone else in the pub, I joined in the chorus. Later, Anthony came down and I introduced both Pat and Lynn to him.

The evening was very special, as that night there were two young women step dancers who performed with Anora. My daughters were mesmerized by their performance. It was a lovely, very memorable evening.

Pat and Lynn are each unique. Pat would never be described as shy or self-effacing; she's assertive and fearless. She tells the story of one time, in Benton Harbor, going to a small mom-and-pop place not far from the house on her brand-new Schwinn bicycle. She left it outside briefly while she went in to buy herself a treat. When she came out, her bike was gone. She was furious. And determined to get it back. She set out on a citywide search-and-recovery mission.

At one point she found herself wandering down a dimly lit alley. There in the gloom she encountered a big black man. He ran a small BBQ place there. He asked her what she was doing, and she told him somebody had stolen her bike, and she was looking for the person who did it so she could take it back. It was late in the day, and the man was concerned about her safety. So he let her use his phone to call me. I went down and picked her up. She was still angry and insistent that she was going to find her bike. Unfortunately, she never did.

Lynn, on the other hand, was rather shy and soft spoken. She was the yin to Pat's yang. I remembered one night when I was chief of police in Portland, this during the "death squad" incident when emotions were running very high. Someone phoned the house while we were in the middle of dinner. Lynn got up and answered the phone.

I couldn't help but overhear her responding to the caller. "Yes...yes. Okay. Thank you for calling."

When she came back to the table, I asked her who had called.

"Some man. I don't know who it was," she answered.

"Well, what did he want?"

"He just called to tell us that he was going to blow up our house."

Ever polite—at times to a fault.

The three of us got along wondrously and talked nonstop the whole time we were together. We talked about the sights we were seeing, the places we visited, and of memories of the earlier trip we'd made with their families two years before.

The girls also reminisced about their growing up, recounting seminal events in their lives.

"Remember in Harvey when we got a puppy, and it bit me in the face and I had to go to the hospital to get stitches?" Lynn asked.

I shook my head. "No. Sweetie, I don't."

"Remember the time in Portland when I broke my foot in the garage and you put me on the back of your motorcycle and drove me to the emergency room at Maine Medical Center?" Pat said.

"I'm sorry, I don't," I replied, pained by the realization that not only had I missed so much of their lives when they were growing up, but that I couldn't even remember such significant events. It was distressing to realize how absorbed I had been in my work, first as an undercover narc, and later as chief of police in three very different cities.

"What about when I had those seizures and you and Mom had to take me to Ann Arbor for special tests?" Lynn asked.

I shook my head. I couldn't believe I had no recollection of that.

At breakfast the morning before we were to leave, Lynn looked around the table at Pat and me and noted we would be leaving to go home the next day. She got teary as she said it. We all did. We all understood just how special our time together had been. It had been unbelievably fabulous—and now that it was drawing to a close, it was achingly bittersweet.

I told them how distressful it was for me to realize how much I had missed out on in their lives. I was sorry for that. Both girls were gracious and kind, insisting that it was okay, that they knew that I was busy with important matters at work. They both stressed that it was important to focus on what we had now, how incredible it was that we'd had this time together—that we all had so much to be grateful for.

On the drive to the airport in Shannon the next morning, the mood was subdued. I dropped them off at the terminal, then returned the rental car before rejoining them to catch our flight back to Boston.

Pat sat across the aisle from Lynn and me, as we had seats together. We all watched in-flight movies and slept some, as our time together had been full, with late evenings out. Throughout the long flight, Lynn and I also talked. I was still feeling bad about the missed opportunities during their growing up, how I should have been more involved, more of a central figure in their lives. Lynn kept insisting that it was okay. That what was most important was to appreciate the moment, to be grateful for all that we do have that binds us as family.

We were met in Boston by Lynn's husband, who came to pick her up and drive her back to Connecticut. It was very emotional saying good-bye. We cheered ourselves with talk of doing the trip again soon.

A driver I'd hired to take me back to Portland was late. Pat and I waited together, then when he arrived, I had him drive over to the terminal where Pat was to catch her flight.

We stood and hugged for a long time. She told me she loved me. Finally, we said good-bye, and I watched her with her luggage disappear into the terminal.

It was a long drive back to Portland. I was glad to be getting home, but I was sad, too, that this most special of special trips with my daughters had come to an end.

I was buoyed, however, by the thought that we had talked about doing it again soon.

I feel very fortunate for the long and varied career that I've had in law enforcement. The arc of the journey isn't one that I could have imagined starting out all those years ago when I first joined the force in Grand Rapids. That journey has carried me from the dark side, working as an undercover narcotics agent, into the light of enlightened community policing, where I was able to institute and nurture the principles I've long held about police work—that it is a public service, and that the police are not to be apart *from* the community, but a part *of* their community.

And I love living in Maine. I've always greatly enjoyed the summers in Maine. But as I've become more involved and invested in teaching, in working with young people, helping guide and mentor them in their studies and careers, I've come to strongly feel that Maine summers are way too long. At this point, I've had thousands of students come through my classrooms, come to see me in my office, and I've had hundreds join me on trips to Ireland. I've been fortunate to watch countless students go on to become officers with police and sheriff's departments all across Maine. I've watched with pride as they've advanced to become detectives and chiefs and head of county sheriff's departments. Not all my students end up in police work. The noted Maine humorist, Bob Marley, was once a student of mine. I remember telling him if he didn't knock off goofing around, he'd never become a policeman. He didn't knock it off, and he didn't become a police officer, but he has gone on to be one of the funniest stand-up comedians in the country—and a Maine treasure.

Some things in my life I wish I'd done differently. Most especially being a more attentive father. I missed so much of my daughters' growing up, missed being more integral to their young lives. They were fortunate that their mother was always there for them. That she gave so generously of herself in raising them. She saw that they both grew into lovely young women—and later loving mothers and wives.

I was a better, more involved father in raising my son, Will. But I'm so fortunate now to have the opportunity to spend more time with Pat and Lynn.

At the end of the shift, at the end of the day, no matter where you are in your career—family is priceless. I'm grateful to have been given a second chance to fully appreciate just how true this is. And to discover that it is never too late for second chances to take that to heart.

ACKNOWLEDGMENTS

Diane Scott—a special friend who has been with me through thick and thin. When contemplating the writing of my life story, I told her I had no idea what the title should be. She thought for a moment, and said *Sonny Days* would be a great title. She was right once again. Thanks, Diane.

Perry Clark, Esq.—a unique man of great intelligence and humor. I asked Perry if he would read a rough draft of the book and give me his opinion. He did, and his thoughts were excellent—as usual. Thanks, Perry.

Carole Ann Dunphe—my wife's dear friend who also read the rough draft and gave sound advice and encouragement. You are one of a kind—in a good way.

I remember always the men and women with whom I have worked over the years in law enforcement agencies. Their sacrifices will never be fully appreciated by the public they served. I will never forget your sacrifices.

Special thanks to all my students. Your uniqueness and interest in learning and self-improvement have made teaching rewarding and a special endeavor. Most importantly, I hope I have passed along to you the belief that you can overcome adversity. Never give up.